APR '98

W9-CLD-287

364.1532 C966r

Cuklanz, Lisa M.

Rape on trial

JAN 0 2 1997
JAN 1 8 1997
JAN 2 4 1998

JUN 1 4 2001
FEB 1 1 2003

APR 2 2 2003

DEMCO 38-297

MAR 5 1996

Rape on Trial

University of Pennsylvania Press
Feminist Cultural Studies, the Media, and Political Culture
Mary Ellen Brown and Andrea Press, Editors

A complete listing of the books in this series
appears at the back of this volume

Rape on Trial

How the Mass Media Construct Legal
Reform and Social Change

Lisa M. Cuklanz

Columbia College Library
600 South Michigan
Chicago, IL 60605

University of Pennsylvania Press

Philadelphia

Grateful acknowledgment is made for permission to reprint material from the following sources:

Hesper Anderson, *Rape and Marriage: The Rideout Case* (teleplay). Copyright © 1980 by Lorimar Productions, Inc. All rights reserved.

Noreen Connell and Cassandra Wilson, editors, *Rape: The First Sourcebook for Women.* Copyright © 1974 by Noreen Connell and Cassandra Wilson. By permission of Dutton Signet, a division of Penguin Books USA, Inc.

Susan Griffin, *Rape: The Politics of Consciousness*, pp. 25, 29, 31–33. Copyright © 1979, 1986 by Susan Griffin. By permission of HarperCollins Publishers, Inc.

Andra Medea and Kathleen Thompson, *Against Rape.* Copyright © 1974 by Noonday Press. By permission of Andra Medea and Kathleen Thompson.

Tom Topor, *The Accused* (screenplay). Copyright © 1995 by Paramount Pictures. By permission of Paramount Pictures.

CBS News transcripts of coverage of the Rideout, Dotson, and New Bedford cases used by permission of CBS News, a division of CBS Inc.

Copyright © 1996 by Lisa M. Cuklanz
All rights reserved
Printed in the United States of America

Library of Congress Cataloging-in-Publication Data
Cuklanz, Lisa M.
    Rape on trial : how the mass media construct legal reform and social change /
Lisa M. Cuklanz.
        p.   cm. — (Feminist cultural studies, the media, and political culture)
    Includes bibliographical references and index.
    ISBN 0-8122-3321-2 (alk. paper). — ISBN 0-8122-1559-1 (pbk. : alk. paper)
      1. Rape in mass media—United States.   2. Rape—Law and legislation—United States.
3. Women—Crimes against—United States.   4. Trials (Rape)—United States.   5. Crime
and the press—United States.   6. United States—Social conditions—1980–
I. Title.   II. Series.
P96.R35C85   1995
364.1′532—dc20   95-24840
                                                                                                              CIP

364.1532 C966r

Cuklanz, Lisa M.

Rape on trial

Contents

Acknowledgments

Before I began this project I had little appreciation for the network of friends, colleagues, mentors, and editors necessary to the production of such a work. Now, after several years of revision, I am happy to have the opportunity to formally thank all those who have had a hand in its development and completion.

This book began in 1989 as a dissertation idea. After completing the dissertation in 1991 under the insightful direction of Michael McGee and with the financial backing of the Jane A. Weiss Memorial Scholarship at the University of Iowa, I began the years-long process of rewriting and refocusing. During this time I was fortunate to have the support of Boston College, whose generous Research Development Grant allowed me to focus entirely on this project for more than three months.

I am also in the debt of Celeste Condit for her unflagging encouragement and for her help in editing various drafts. I thank Kathryn Cirksena for her time and intelligent direction. Special thanks are also owed to Laura X and her Clearinghouse on Marital Rape for help with research on the Rideout case.

This project would not have been possible without the help of many others too numerous to name who read the manuscript at various stages, provided comments and suggestions, and encouraged me to see the project through in spite of the time and energy it required. Credit also goes to the many courthouse clerks, librarians, court reporters, and judicial staff members who were willing to provide valuable information and suggestions for further research.

This book is dedicated to my parents, Harlan and Joyce Cuklanz, who have been unwavering in their encouragement and support.

Chapter 1
Introduction:
Why Famous Rape Trials?

It is almost impossible to tune in to radio or television news or to pick up a newspaper without encountering a story about a trial whose arguments are unfolding in public view. Many of these public trials concern issues of gender: the role of women in traditionally male arenas such as military combat or popular team sports, the treatment or behavior women encounter in entering these spheres, and the progression of women's legal rights to equal pay, equal work, and equal treatment under the law have all made headlines as a result of specific cases. Such cases highlight the significant and problematic nature of gender in contemporary culture and often become the subjects of popular fictions such as films or television specials. Gender issues have gained unprecedented prominence in our national discourses of politics, economics, and law. Is all this discussion moving us any closer to agreement or equality? The discussion of public trials is an important arena for airing arguments on all sides of controversial subjects, and national-level discourse on such issues enacts a sort of compromise between opposing viewpoints on issues of broad significance.

For several decades now, dedicated women and men have worked to eradicate the inequities in rape laws that once treated victims as criminals. Thousands of survivors of rape have testified to the profound dehumanization of trials that placed them under scrutiny, and thousands have worked to reform both laws and attitudes that rendered rape a virtually unpunishable offense. Scholars, researchers, reformers, politicians, and crisis workers have pooled their efforts to give voice to the painful experiences of women who for centuries found little justice within the judicial system. At present, many questions remain: To what extent have these efforts to be heard been successful? What is the process by which marginal ideas about rape have become mainstream? When, and to what extent, are we as a culture being asked to listen to women's perspectives on rape? What issues are being represented as the significant or relevant elements of this experience? This book examines public discourses surrounding famous rape trials as the arena within which the struggle for a feminist understanding of rape has been fought.

The story of rape law reform concerns women's efforts to name and describe their experiences of rape and the ensuing rape trials and to have these experiences legitimated in legal statutes. However, although statutes in many states were changed years ago, the power of traditional ideas about rape has limited the acceptance of feminist ideas beyond the legal realm. The silencing of groups and individuals who wish to speak against established practices, beliefs, policies, and definitions is central to the maintenance of existing power relations. This silencing takes place at all stages in the struggle for social change, even after laws have been enacted to give voice to previously unheard groups. Discovering and exposing the means by which people are silenced are the first steps in the effort to oppose and resist them.

For women, these discoveries have been especially important. Women's claiming of public voice has been for centuries of the utmost importance in their fight to attain status as full citizens in Western culture. The desire to maintain and expand that public voice has continued to grow as women have become increasingly aware that female, feminine, and feminist perspectives are often distorted by or eliminated from public discussion of even those issues and policies that affect women most. Although significant gains have been made for women as speakers and actors in the public sphere, and although there are no longer legal statutes that limit female speech and participation in the public realm, there nonetheless remain powerful elements of resistance to the expression of women's experiences, beliefs, and feelings, particularly when such experiences appear to deviate from accepted norms.

The movement for rape law reform grew not only out of a general feminist project of legal reform, but also out of specific experiences and analyses of the traditional conduct of rape trials. Rape claimants prior to 1970 were routinely asked to prove that they were of perfect moral character, while defense attorneys dredged through the victims' sexual histories to show otherwise. Activists observed a conviction rate for rape that was practically negligible. In New York City in 1971, for example, the conviction rate for rape was three-tenths of one percent (Connell and Wilson 1974, 128). At the same time, women began to talk about their experiences of, and reactions to, rape and to understand this crime in systemic as well as personal terms:

Conditioned to believe that the rapist was sick and a social aberration, while at the same time held accountable for attracting and precipitating the sexual violence we often experienced, many women repressed their memories of rape. . . . But as women compared their experiences they began to come to some understanding of the anger they had kept hidden even from themselves. The pattern that emerged from their individual experiences was not a common pattern of assault . . . but a common pattern of responses that they encountered—"You're lying," "It was your fault," "You should have been more careful," "You're exaggerating." Through the process of consciousness-raising, women moved on from the discovery that sexual assault was not just an individual and unique experience to the realization that rape, as an issue, was a means of analyzing the psychological and political structures of oppression in our society. (Connell and Wilson 1974, 3)

What began as consciousness-raising among victims of rape soon expanded to an effort to gain a more public, collective voice to articulate the victim's experiences of both the rape and the rape trial. In particular, feminists began to question the social and legal practice of blaming the victim. They developed an analysis of rape that placed the blame on rapists and on the culture that produced them, and worked to change laws and attitudes to reflect this new understanding.

The first formal legislation to incorporate the new feminist understanding was the Michigan statute passed in 1974. It served as a model for other states throughout the following decade. The Michigan statute gave new weight to the perspective of the female victim. It eliminated the requirement for corroborating testimony (which was not required for any other felony), barred sexual history evidence because of its irrelevance to consent or motive, and developed a graduated scale of sexual assault crimes to increase the chance of conviction for rapes and sexual assaults that were less than horrific attacks accompanied by severe physical abuse. Although the revised statutes signified the public legitimacy of a female perspective on rape, and although most states have passed some version of a reformed statute, many observers and activists still wonder whether a female voice can ever achieve legitimacy outside the legal codes, in the public discourse and beliefs surrounding rape.

Over the last ten years there has been much speculation and dispute concerning the impact of the American feminist movement of the past three decades. Both academic and popular press discussions suggest or assert outright that this movement has failed or run aground. Susan Faludi's 1991 book, *Backlash: The Undeclared War Against American Women*, documents the pervasive popular press assertion that the movement has ended, failed, and/or lost the attention of younger women. In this national bestseller, Faludi notes that many women believe that the chance for substantial change has been lost as the feminist movement has died out (Faludi 1991, 58). Similarly, observers supportive of the more specific movement for rape law reform have noted the discouraging limitations encountered in that arena. By the early 1980s nearly all states had considered or passed reform legislation, yet trial practice had changed so little that Susan Estrich was led to wonder whether the primary contribution of reform legislation had been simply to prevent questions about the victim's sexual history (Estrich 1987, 80). Clearly, the goals of the larger feminist movement and the rape law reform movement have met with significant roadblocks: "There were changes: the laws changed; courtroom procedures changed; police procedures changed. Still, and here we might fall under the shadow of defeat and say, nothing has really changed . . . even if these conditions are not natural like earthquakes or tornadoes, even if rape is an unnatural occurrence, the truth is, the force of society is too great, the force of habit too deep" (Griffin 1979, 31). The limitations rape law reform advocates encountered in their attempt to redefine traditional cultural conceptions of rape and its victims can be seen as evidence that the power to silence is still salient; yet the opposing argument, that feminists have obtained significant voice for the experiences of rape victims, can be supported as well.

Clearly, modern feminism is not a failure, having made immeasurable progress by establishing women's studies, by directly affecting legal statutes, and by developing a proliferation of materials by, for, and about women. The question of the success or failure of social movements has been made both complex and interesting in part because of the ability of contemporary institutions to accommodate, coopt, and redefine efforts at social change. The transformation of the goals and efforts of any social movement is to be expected, as it is widely acknowledged that hegemonic forces such as the mass media work to reinforce the myths that comprise dominant ideology, rendering current relations of power logical or even natural.

What has not been fully explored are the ways in which these conservative forces have done the work of diverting, fragmenting, and sabotaging the public, particularly mass-mediated, expression of female perspectives on rape in recent years. Yet, the terms of media discussions do change, and as representatives of mainstream thought, such discussions deserve examination, for they can provide a useful measure of social change. One of the most important indicators of the effort's success is reflected in the content of public consciousness: Do our mainstream discussions of rape include or take into account the new feminist formulations of rape? Or have new laws merely provided a secluded arena for their expression? In short, to what extent has this movement succeeded in articulating to a nationwide audience new points of view, new truths about rape victims' experiences? These questions can best be answered through a careful analysis of the treatment of rape in the mythic narratives of our time. Mainstream news texts and popular fiction constitute two sources of such mythic narratives.

Contemporary social movement theorists are well aware that efforts such as the rape law reform movement may be successful without necessarily achieving all of their original agendas (see Touraine 1988). Scholars of the social change movements of the sixties posited an "agitation and response" model that emphasized strategies, tactics, and their specific efficacy in obtaining change (Bowers and Ochs 1971). Currently, language systems, subjectivity, and discursive practices are recognized as important areas of change that can indicate shifts at the level of individual awareness or cultural recognition. Such influences are difficult to measure and discuss, but are nonetheless profound and significant: a movement may achieve some degree of success simply by labeling a previously unspoken problem or phenomenon, such as sexual harassment or marital rape, even if the movement as a whole fails to achieve its original "goals." Gradually, movements that at the outset demanded revolutionary change have been coopted or coerced into a less revolutionary stance, but they nonetheless have influenced the interpretations, meanings, and experiences available within traditional structures and processes. If public discussions about rape have changed to include expressions of the victim's perspective, this may constitute significant social change, even if the incidence of rape has not declined.

For feminist rape reform efforts, public expression is in itself a significant achievement, as Susan Griffin notes: "But now, as equally strongly as I know, without statistics, that violence against women continues, I also know we have not failed; we are not defeated. I do not *feel* defeated . . . and now I can tell you what it felt like to hear [a journalist and rape victim] speak out about this rape. A kind of opening of the field. This terror, this subjection, this humiliation and torture, she said, we will not bear" (Griffin 1979, 32–33). Griffin further states that speaking out "in itself is healing" and that "the change we have wrought is a change in consciousness" (Griffin 1979, 33). To speak, to have a public voice, and to be able to redefine and rename have historically been hard-won entitlements for women. These expressions have always taken place within a context where the dissemination of feminist ideas has been limited by the dominant patriarchal culture.

Theorists of ideology and hegemony have long understood the elasticity that characterizes entrenched systems of politics, education, and meaning in the face of efforts toward change. This adaptability has been variously labeled "containment," "cooptation," and "adjustment," referring to the dominant power's tendency to turn impulses and meanings away from their original course and toward the maintenance of current understandings, beliefs, and especially practices. Thus, despite feminism's articulation of new ideas based on the victim's experience, rape continues at an alarming rate. In 1990, more than one hundred rapes in a population 100,000 were reported to police, up from eighty-three per 100,000 in 1980 ("Crimes and Crime Rates by Type," *U.S. Statistical Abstracts* 1992). In addition, attitudes that enable and even encourage rape continue to find expression in mainstream culture. In large part, then, the battle of rape law reform has not ended with changes in legal statutes, but rather extends necessarily into the realm of public communication and consciousness. This book examines, on the level of public discourse, the actual struggles for social change that occur beyond the legal victories or defeats, for it is on this rhetorical terrain that much real social change takes place.

Beyond legal change, the important battle is what John Fiske acknowledges as the "struggle both to construct a [sense of] reality and to circulate that reality as widely and smoothly as possible throughout society" (Fiske 1989, 150). This book explores the give and take of the specific cultural terrain where a system of power is directly challenged by forces of change. Nationally publicized discussions of noncelebrity rape trials serve as an important forum for this struggle. In this study, certain highly publicized rape trials can be seen both as a means through which feminist meanings are curtailed or delimited and as a vehicle through which these reinterpreted feminist ideas are broadcast to the general culture. This book explicates the interplay between containment and transformation of cultural knowledge of rape through an examination of three issue-oriented trial events. These events—the rape trials of John Rideout, six New Bedford, Massachusetts, bar patrons, and Gary Dotson[1]—provide material for examining in detail the extent to which the victim's perspective on rape has been publicly validated. Further, they afford an opportunity to examine the process of social change, the alteration of dominant ideology, as it incorporates some elements of feminist truth about rape. The emphasis is on the struggle for meaning that is acted out in mainstream texts: at various points and in differing texts both traditional and reform voices have gained discursive authority. Public communication about rape is central to the study of the effectiveness of the rape reform movement because only this examination can reveal the extent to which the movement has altered the public consciousness.

Trials as Subjects of Public Discourse on Rape

The primary focus of debate over voice and interpretation of rape has clearly been the court trial. For many women, the trial becomes a "second rape," where survivors are forced to relive their painful experiences and to justify their actions and personal histories (Madigan and Gamble 1989; Savage 1990). The positioning of the trial as a significant public site of struggle over meanings about rape can also be seen through the disproportionate emphasis given to rape trials by mainstream news media. Between 1974 and 1991, more than half of all coverage of rape indexed in both the *New York Times Index* and the *Readers Guide to Periodical Literature* focused on specific trials. In short, there have been many heavily reported trials involving rape, and most of the stories about rape have centered on particular trials. Theories of ideology and hegemony have been applied to the mass media by other scholars, but these concepts have yet to be employed in the emerging area of rhetorical and media scholarship on "popular trials" (Hariman 1990). When these trials deal with rape, they reveal whose voice is being heard, in what ways and on what issues. When most public discussion of rape centers on a few highly publicized trials, the trials become central to the process of accommodation by which the dominant ideology shifts to cope with feminist challenges. An examination of the terms in which these trials have been discussed will reveal how ideas of change have been accepted, transformed, coopted, suppressed, or rejected by dominant discourses.

Highly publicized trials are in one sense vehicles of control and containment, yet they are also the trumpet calls that bring attention to the issues they involve. Through discussions of rape trials, the climate of public opinion has been adjusted to a slight degree as writers and observers have attempted to adjudicate between a traditional view of rape and a revision based on female experience and voice. This process is underway whenever trials dealing with gender or other contemporary social subjects reach national mainstream news outlets.

Issue-Oriented Rape Cases in the National Media

Nine cases involving rape have received significant news coverage since rape law reform began in 1974. The first involved Joan Little, a prison inmate tried for killing a prison guard with a pick after an attempted rape. The Inez Garcia case also involved the killing of a rapist after the fact. Garcia was convicted at the first trial but was acquitted on the basis of self-defense on appeal. These were murder trials rather than rape trials and are worthy of comparative study and analysis. They are not, however, part of the scope of this book, which focuses specifically on rape trials that received sustained national attention. While both the Little and Garcia cases gained some national coverage, this was in each case limited to a few items in the *New York Times* and a handful of magazine articles. A third case involving rape that is not part of this analysis is the Central Park "wilding" case of 1989, which did receive sustained national attention but was for the most part covered as a rampage and brutal attack rather than as a rape.[2] Again, this latter point is worthy of extended study, but it renders the case less central to the project of this book than are the three selected cases. In effect, the "issue" in the Central Park case was not depicted as rape, but rather as some intersection of race, violence, and inner-city life.

As celebrity trials, the William Kennedy-Smith and Mike Tyson cases both received national attention because of the identity of the parties involved. Chapter 3 discusses the importance for cultural analysis of treating celebrity cases as distinct from other issue-oriented trials. Finally, the recent (1993) New Jersey case involving several teenage boys who were convicted of raping a retarded neighbor certainly offered contested social understandings of rape. This case will be important for future study of rape trials but, again, it is outside the scope of this analysis.

The Rideout, Big Dan's, and Dotson cases were chosen for extensive coverage by the national media *because they dealt with rape.* The characteristics of these cases place them at the intersection of current scholarship on "popular" trials and the study of social movements' engagement with the dominant culture; as such, they are the central focus of this book. In addition, each of the three cases to be examined here was the subject of a subsequent fictional text, and thus they offer three opportunities to examine a complex, step-by-step adjustment in public discourse through the comparative study of news media accounts and the fictionalized texts that were created after each trial. The practice of creating fictionalized accounts of famous trials is increasingly prevalent—a further sign of the significance of discursive struggle in the process of social change.

These rewritten stories offer an excellent opportunity for comparison with news coverage, but perhaps more importantly, they also indicate that the trial verdict is not the end of the story: the fictionalized narratives restructured elements of the story as told by the news media, repositioning the characters and drawing different inferences about truth, innocence, and guilt. In each case, themes from news coverage were also picked up or even expanded. The terms of this revision are explored here, again with special focus on traditional and reformed ideas about rape. This detailed comparative analysis of news and fictional discourses surrounding a particular type of rape trial illustrates the differential functions of news and mass-mediated fiction in both maintaining and altering widespread assumptions, functions these two discourses are likely to perform in their treatments of other subjects as well. The selection and coverage of certain cases and the subsequent retelling of the story in new terms is a process commonly undertaken in U.S. culture. This process facilitates the negotiation of social change in graduated steps that can stretch out over many years, but which publicly move toward change in increasingly broad measures.

The Rideout Case

The Rideout marital rape case received public attention from 1978, when pretrial proceedings were picked up by national newswriters, through 1980, when a CBS movie-of-the-week based on the case was first aired. In 1977 the Oregon legislature became one of three state legislatures to remove the traditional common law exemption which held that husbands could not rape their wives. Many states already allowed wives to charge their husbands with rape provided that the two were legally separated, but in Oregon a husband living with his wife could be charged. John Rideout became the first man in the United States to be so charged when his wife Greta accused him of rape during a period when they were "cohabiting." The Rideouts' marriage was troubled and had become increasingly violent. One afternoon, John Rideout prevented his wife from escaping their home by tampering with her car; he chased her down outside their apartment and led her back inside. John and Greta told different stories from this point. He admitted hitting her in the face and causing bruises, but claimed they made up and then engaged in consensual intercourse. She alleged that he hit and threatened her until she was afraid to continue resisting. The trial lasted four days, and John was acquitted. The Rideouts were reconciled a few weeks later for a brief period, but they later separated and then divorced. Subsequently John was arrested and convicted of breaking into Greta's apartment, a crime for which he spent two months in jail. Greta stayed separated from John permanently after this episode, although many news sources reported only the earlier reconciliation and not the permanent divorce.

The case gained national attention before coming to trial, sparking dozens of articles and editorials and attracting the attention of such syndicated columnists as William Raspberry, George Will, Ellen Goodman, and Carl Rowan. It was picked up by the *New York Times* and by national newsmagazines, and was covered daily throughout the proceedings by local newspapers. ABC, CBS, and NBC also covered the trial and updated the story throughout the following year. John and Greta appeared on *Good Morning America,* and their experiences were used as the basis for a 1980 CBS movie-of-the-week, *Rape and Marriage: The Rideout Case.*

The Big Dan's Case

On a March night in 1983 a young woman entered a bar to buy cigarettes. She stayed for a drink and talked with the only other woman in the bar, a waitress. As she prepared to leave, she was prevented from exiting by two men who carried her to a pool table and raped her with the help of several other men.

In 1984, the Big Dan's Tavern rape in New Bedford, Massachusetts, came to trial. Televised on CNN, it was to be the most highly publicized of the three trials. Media emphasis on the ethnic background of the six defendants, the number of men involved, and the dehumanizing brutality of the crime was intense enough that questions as to whether there could be a fair trial were raised by the defense attorneys. The trial was moved to a nearby town. Two separate trials were held on the same days, since the defendants were accused of different offenses and since the testimony of some implicated others. Witnesses, including the victim, testified at one trial in the morning and another in the afternoon. Four defendants were convicted of varying charges and two were acquitted. The gang rape in Big Dan's bar involved Portuguese immigrant defendants, and the victim and district attorney were also members of the Portuguese-American community of New Bedford. These facts were of central importance in news accounts.

After national CNN coverage and local newspapers publicized her name, the victim was subjected to continued threats and harassment; she ultimately changed her identity and left town. Taped copies of CNN coverage are "unavailable" from CNN because the trial was so long ago (1984).[3] This case also was reported on extensively by the *New York Times* and by all three network news sources (from the initial announcement of the rape to the final verdict). Nationally circulated newsmagazines such as *Time* and *Newsweek* also covered the case, as did local papers such as the *Providence Journal* and the *Boston Globe*. In 1985, the made-for-TV movie *Silent Witness*, based on the barroom rape, was released, followed in 1988 by the Hollywood film *The Accused*, "inspired by" the events of the New Bedford rape (although this film carried the disclaimer that any similarity to a "real" case was purely coincidental). Jodie Foster received an Academy Award for her performance as the rape victim, fictionally named Sarah Tobias.

The Webb-Dotson Case

In 1985 a third rape case reached a national audience and provoked discussion about social values and gender roles. In April of that year, Cathleen Crowell Webb came forward with the assertion that her testimony of 1979, largely responsible for Gary Dotson's conviction and lengthy sentence for rape, was entirely fabricated. Webb had testified in 1979 that she had been kidnapped by three men and raped in the back seat of a car by Gary Dotson, whom she had identified from police mug shots as well as in a subsequent lineup. (Webb had also selected a close friend of Dotson's from the mug shots but was less certain about his participation in the rape.) She had previously described her assailant with such accuracy that there was a remarkable resemblance between the resultant police artist's sketch and Dotson's photograph. In 1985 Webb claimed to have "faked" the rape by bruising herself, cutting herself on the abdomen with a glass bottle, ripping her clothing, and stumbling along an unlit road. She further claimed that she had invented the story because she feared pregnancy after intercourse with her boyfriend.

Webb's recantation caused a groundswell of popular support for Dotson, who, Webb proclaimed, had been falsely imprisoned on the basis of her earlier testimony. After Judge Richard Samuels, the original judge in the case, heard the recanted testimony and sent Dotson back to prison, the popular outcry—in the form of petition drives and phone calls to the attorneys involved (see Boyce 1985) —was so strong that Governor James Thompson of Illinois agreed to hold a nationally televised special clemency hearing, after which he also concluded that Dotson was indeed guilty. However, allegedly in order to maintain confidence in the Illinois justice system, he commuted Dotson's sentence to time already served. Dotson's name was not cleared until his formal pardon in 1989, which was based on revised DNA analysis of the semen and blood stains from the 1979 evidence.

Webb and Dotson appeared together on all three broadcast networks' morning news programs, and Webb published a book titled *Forgive Me* in 1985. The case was covered extensively in the *Chicago Tribune* and the *New York Times*, and national newsmagazines such as *Time* and *Newsweek* and popular magazines such as *People* published articles on the events. All three television networks covered the case throughout the hearings and decisions. Highly publicized plans for a television movie or miniseries and a book about Dotson's experiences were never realized. According to Webb's coauthored book, she received forty-one movie offers but refused to profit from her experiences in the case.

*   *   *

In an era of heightened awareness of gender roles, rape, and rape law reform, how has the national publicity afforded these trials in news and fiction brought about change in dominant ideology? Likewise, how has this discussion limited, redefined, or diverted discussion of issues important to victims of rape and their supporters? The creation of these news events is an important step in the process through which rape reform ideas are accepted into mainstream consciousness about rape. In effect, news coverage of these cases enacts the acceptance of certain feminist ideas into dominant ideology, and this enactment can be documented by analyzing news coverage in two of these three cases. At the same time, however, mainstream news coverage also functions to reject other rape reform ideas.

The fictionalized representations of these cases in many ways mirror the news coverage, but they also serve a more important function in the process of ideological accommodation: it is in this realm that feminist perspectives can be given further legitimacy and articulation.

Chapter 2 traces the legitimization in legal writings of traditional understandings of rape drawn from English common law and presents beliefs proposed as a coherent set of reform alternatives. Chapter 3 identifies the new genre of the highly publicized trial, discussing its discursive contributions to the process of social change in contemporary culture and situating each of the three cases introduced above within this new genre. Chapter 4 examines the news discourse surrounding each trial. News values that make trials "news" also work to contain and/or exclude reformed understandings of rape, but in two of the three cases one important aspect of the victim's experience was incorporated into mainstream "truth" about rape. Chapter 5 turns to the fictional portrayals of each case to show how these fictional narratives represent a second step in the process of ideological shift by picking up and focusing on issues central to news while also allowing for further acceptance of the victim's perspective and further articulation of feminist ideas about rape.

This book explicates the specific means by which popular discourse both resisted and accepted reform understandings of rape and illuminates the step-by-step process that has unfolded over the last two decades as our culture has shifted its understanding of the truth about this important contemporary social issue. The changes in mainstream discourse documented here represent the profound accomplishments that established a public voice for the victims of rape—accomplishments that represent the success of feminist efforts to redefine knowledge and truth about common human experiences.

Notes

1. Strictly speaking, coverage of the Dotson case examined here did not involve a rape "trial." Dotson was convicted in a 1979 trial that received negligible media attention. The media coverage discussed here began in 1985 when the victim, Cathleen Crowell Webb, recanted her 1979 testimony. Public hearings and press conferences ensued, keeping the case in the national spotlight for several weeks. This case provided an important forum for the public discussion of rape and as such deserves attention.

2. I do not argue that this case offers nothing of interest with respect to rape, but rather that this case did not provoke significant public discussion in which the meaning of rape was contested. For a detailed analysis of the intersection of race and gender in news coverage of this case, see Helen Benedict's *Virgin or Vamp: How the Press Covers Sex Crimes* (New York: Oxford University Press, 1992), chapter 6.

3. Taped segments of the televised trial are available at the Harvard Law School Library audiovisual department. Trial transcript quotes in the following text are based on the printed transcript rather than the tapes.

Chapter 2
A Particular Social Reality:
Rape Law and Rape Law Reform

> . . . much of what was the actuality of our lives went unnamed.
> We did not speak of rape. If a woman was raped she was supposed
> to feel ashamed. She was shamed. The very atmosphere around her
> said she must have wanted this rape, drawn this to her. And the
> atmosphere, like rape itself, seemed as if it had existed forever, were
> a natural phenomenon, and not made up of man-made assumptions
> and prejudices born of a particular social reality.
>
> (Griffin 1979, 25)

Prior to the 1970s, U.S. rape law, based on traditional rape myths and
laws passed down from centuries of British history, focused on protect-
ing the accused rapist against allegedly dishonest, vengeful, and even
psychopathic "claimants" of rape. Social and religious conventions made
a woman's chastity important to her marriageability, which was directly
linked to her economic survival. In this context, lawmakers assumed
that pressures on women to bring false accusations of rape were great,
since only a claim of rape could even partially rescue an "unchaste"
woman from infamy and poverty. In light of the great value placed on
women's premarital virginity, the British (and later American) legal system prescribed severe punishment, including the death penalty, for rape
convictions. In the United States, this severe penalty was also fueled
by racist beliefs that assumed that Black and other nonwhite men were
most likely rapists, and that white women were the most frequent victims. From a white male perspective, severe punishments served both to
protect white women and to deter potential rapists.

Rape mythology grew out of the beliefs and fears of those who had
the power to write and enforce laws. A cluster of mutually reinforcing

myths combined to produce a "rational" system of belief. Over time, these myths were incorporated into case law and legal opinion, reifying the perspective of upper-class white men. In the early 1970s, female rape victims began to share their experiences with each other and to realize that their ordeals were not reflected in legal and social knowledge about rape. They embarked upon an organized effort to change both statutes and cultural beliefs.

The rape law reform movement in the United States, as the name clearly indicates, has aimed at changing legal definitions, statutes, and processes related to rape. Rape law reformers have sought to alter social understandings of rape that either originated with or were firmly entrenched in the law. An important step in this process, they believed, was to alter official definitions within statutes in the hopes that both legal practice and social comprehension would change following the new laws. As with all feminist movements in the latter half of this century, the success of rape law reform would depend in part upon the ability of reformers to offer new concepts of female and male nature, and in part on the degree to which these new concepts were accepted by the larger culture. Thus, although they focused their initial energies on changing laws, reformers realized that their larger project involved an effort to radically alter popular understandings of how and why women and men act in particular ways in particular situations.

As Susan Griffin, Susan Estrich, and many others have observed, rape reform has been successful if measured in terms of statutory changes. The movement has been less completely successful in disseminating and gaining acceptance for revised understandings of rape and in reducing the incidence of rape in the United States. Popular fiction continues to portray reluctant and resistant women "changing their minds" and enjoying sex after being forced into it. Rape statistics continue to escalate rather than decline. Statistics for reported rapes in the United States show a steady increase since 1982, from 78,800 in 1983 to 102,600 in 1990. The one exception to this steady rise was a drop of 400 reported rapes between the years 1986 and 1987 ("Crimes and Crime Rates by Type," *U.S. Statistical Abstracts 1992,* 180). New definitions have gained some acceptance, but there remain significant obstacles to the elimination or even reduction of the crime itself. This chapter describes both the traditional and feminist frameworks for understanding rape, providing specific issues for reference in subsequent chapters.

The rape law reform movement has existed alongside the concerted efforts of feminists, social workers, sociologists, and others to reexamine and redefine the traditional legal and cultural constructions of rape. Thus, at the same time that law reformers have worked to change statutes, scholars and writers from several fields have taken up a similar project of redefinition aimed at consciousness-raising. Susan Brown-miller's book *Against Our Will: Men, Women, and Rape* (1975) was one of the most widely read works among an initial explosion of books and monographs critical of traditional views of rape (see Medea and Thompson 1974; Russell 1975; Connell and Wilson 1974; Horos 1974; Hursch 1977; MacKellar 1975). These writers, like the legal reformers, sought to explain how ideas about rape helped to maintain gender oppression. Whereas in previous decades the subject of rape had been consistently sparse in law publications (four to six law review monographs per year), the number of articles mushroomed after 1975. By 1977 seventy-four law review articles and numerous books had been published on the subject (the number of law review articles published jumped from seven in 1974 to twenty-one in 1975). Of course, Brownmiller's book did not trigger this intensified interest in rape but rather was an early indicator of a larger trend in changing attitudes about gender in American society. Although her book was controversial because it argued that rape was a necessary element in the patriarchal control of women throughout history, the topic of rape was already being examined. *Against Our Will* appeared just one year after the passage of the reformed Michigan rape statute, and it helped fuel an international effort in the United States, Canada, Great Britain, and Australia to reform social and legal attitudes toward rape, rapists, and rape victims.

In the next five years, more than four dozen books on the subject were published in the United States in the fields of sociology, law, and psychology (see, for example, Holmstrom and Burgess 1978; Eyman 1980; Sanders 1980; Griffin 1979; Gager and Schurr 1976; Hilberman 1976; Walker and Brodsky 1976; Martin 1976). Although a theoretical dispute over the functions and causes of rape emerged from these studies (see Baron and Strauss 1989), they disagreed very little on the questions of what should be counted as rape, who could and did commit rape, and how victims of rape were treated unfairly. Almost invariably, these books began with brief discussion of the "myths" or "misconceptions" about rape, which the authors felt needed to be dispelled and replaced in the minds of readers. In addition, each work supplied alternative "facts" with which to replace the old "myths."

These books serve, then, as a clear and concise record of long ac-cepted "facts" about rape, renamed "rape myths," that were considered common knowledge prior to the early 1970s. They mark a conscious and public attempt by social change activists and scholars to alter the defini-tion of rape by relegating the old definition to the status of myth while advancing their own ideas based on new understandings of the nature of male and female sexuality, the acts involved in the crime of rape, and the basic characteristics or characters of rapists and victims. Most significantly, they began to broaden the categories of people who might be considered rapists or victims by arguing against the restrictive definitions long legitimized in English common law and in American legal scholarship and practice. These were the same definitional struggles faced by feminist law reformers:

In our actions we went right to the sorest wounds. The stories we heard of women who, after being raped, were hounded by police in a kind of inquisition as if the woman had provoked the rape, created a terrible pain in us. . . . After numerous speak-outs were held, in which women stood up and told of having been raped, and then abused by the police and the judicial system, after giving ourselves the so desperately needed time to speak about a long hidden injury, we worked to change these more outrageous injustices inflicted on us by the very system which claimed to protect us. (Griffin 1979, 29)

Rape reformers began to bring their private and semi-private conversations into the public discourse and to legitimize the terms of their discussions in legal statutes. After centuries of representing the fears of powerful male lawmakers, the legal system began to incorporate and thereby validate the experience of women.

This chapter examines five of the myths discussed during the 1975 "publication explosion" and traces their history and maintenance in professional and academic legal discourse prior to 1970, noting both the stability and the adaptability of these myths during decades and even centuries of changing sex roles. Although these definitions probably did not originate in the law, it is there that they received an undeniable stamp of legitimacy and veracity, and it is there that rape reformers focused their energies in the hopes that female experiences of rape could one day become as well understood as the experiences that had fostered traditional beliefs about rape.

Legally Sanctioned Beliefs About Rape Prior to 1970

Legal and social attitudes about the necessary characteristics of rapists and rape victims, as well as characterizations of the crime itself, were remarkably stable from the mid-seventeenth century until the early 1970s. During this lengthy period rape served different social functions in different communities (see D'Emilio and Freedman 1988; Porter 1986; Brownmiller 1975), but the processes and criteria for determining blame and the guilt or innocence of a rapist remained relatively stable. Traditional ideas about rape developed under circumstances in which women were considered the property of their husbands and wherein their chastity determined their value; rape thus constituted theft from a husband or father. From the early 1800s English law books on evidence argued the appropriateness of questioning the rape victim's general "reputation for chastity" as relevant to the issue of consent. Although the defendant was presumed innocent until proven guilty, the victim's claim was under suspicion until she was proven to have the narrowly defined characteristics of chastity and virtue that could then establish her as a "legitimate victim" of rape.

Benedict identifies eight factors—derived from the traditional myths outlined here—that news accounts have used to portray victims as illegitimate claimants (Benedict 1992, 19). These myths, speaking directly to the supposed character of both victim and rapist, formed a system of beliefs in which the victim was put through a trial experience often labeled a "second rape": details of her sexual history, evidence of her chastity, and her motive for alleging rape were called into question in order to impeach her testimony (see Estrich 1987, chapter 1).

The victim's experience of the trial, along with a very low conviction rate even in cases where extreme violence was used, motivated reformers to examine statutes to provide balance at trial. Feminists noted that under the traditional system there was every incentive for victims not to report rapes. One writer noted that rape claimants were often treated poorly through every phase of the investigation, from the hospital examination to the reliving of the rape in court. In addition, victims were expected to have put up the utmost resistance against attack to demonstrate nonconsent; while the defendant's background might not be admissible in court, the victim's sexual history could be used to raise doubts about her testimony; and victims could not retain lawyers but might be faced with an overworked or apathetic prosecutor (Hilberman 1976, 15).

How did legal scholars and practitioners rationalize the traumatic treatment of rape victims at trial? Rape law reformers found that since ideas about the nature of women were at the foundation of legal conceptualizations, reforming the law would entail a change in fundamental beliefs about women and their role in society, a change that would have to incorporate women's subjectivity into the law. To the extent that the discourses of news and fiction surrounding trials can be said to have addressed the issues of change central to rape law reform, these discourses had to take up, discuss, and to some extent reproduce or portray reform alternatives to these long-held conceptions about rape. To the extent that these issues were ignored or afforded minimal attention, the popular discourses failed to address the central issues of rape law reform.

The Special Nature of Rape

Certainly the most long-standing myth about rape is that, because of its sexual and gendered nature, rape is essentially different from all other crimes. This belief has been accompanied by the notion that since rape is an especially heinous crime, accused rapists could expect little sympathy or pity from juries or the public at large. Thus special protections, in the form of unusual trial practices, were allowed in cases of rape. Special jury instructions, required corroboration in cases of rape, and the admissibility of a wide latitude of acceptable "character" evidence were standard practices during rape trials until the mid-1970s.

The legitimacy of these tactics can be traced to Sir Matthew Hale's beliefs about rape, which are so well known that hardly any legal discussion of rape is without reference to his pronouncement that juries should be cautioned about the special nature of the crime. Hale warned: "It is true rape is a most detestable crime, and therefore ought severely and impartially to be punished with death; but it must be remembered, that it is an accusation easily to be made and hard to be proved, and harder to be defended by the party accused, tho never so innocent" (Hale [1650] 1847, 635). Hale's belief in the unreliability of rape victim testimony formally established the legal assumptions that rape victims were more likely to be liars than other witnesses or victims of violent crime, and that the charge of rape was more difficult to prove than other crimes.

In Hale's time, women had strong, socially based motivations to lie about rape. In a footnote, Hale related (but did not document the frequency of) cases in which "the parties being discovered *in coitu*, the woman makes a false charge in order to save her character" (628). At a time when a woman's character was so closely related to her reputation for chastity, some women may have chosen the false accusation of rape, as Hale suggested. Hale cited one case in which this was the final judgment of the court. His ideas were reflected in English common law for the next three centuries, where both corroborating evidence of rape and unusually strict standards of victim credibility had to be met in order to sustain a charge of rape.

Hale's statement about the unusual nature of this crime also continued to be cited routinely *as fact* in United States legal journals until 1969, and his separation of rape from other crimes, with respect to the possibility of false and frivolous accusations, remained a constant concern of police investigators, medical practitioners, and legal and social science scholars through the mid-1970s.

Feminist law reformers in the early 1970s argued that social roles had changed significantly and that this shift warranted a change in the legal disposition toward rape: rape was no longer "special" by dint of its likelihood of false accusation. Since a woman's reputation for chastity no longer determined her economic survival, there no longer existed a compelling reason for a woman to "cry rape." In addition, there had never been any evidence that false accusations of rape were any more likely to result in convictions than false accusations of any other crime. According to reformers, the fear of false accusation, and its supposed consequences for innocent men, had resulted in exaggerated claims about victims of rape as well as in unusual trial practices that further disadvantaged them.

Prior to the mid-1970s, conviction rates for rape were abysmal. Brownmiller analyzed arrest, trial, and conviction statistics, noting that in approximately 85 percent of reported rapes police believed the victim. Of these cases, 51 percent of the rapists were caught, and of these 76 percent were brought to trial. Finally, of this final group, 47 percent ended with the acquittal of the defendant or the dismissal of the case (Brownmiller 1975, 175). Brownmiller added that in some areas of the United States this process whittled down the conviction rate to only 3 percent. An even lower rate was reported in the state of New York, where corroboration was required to prove penetration (Connell and Wilson 1974, 128).

Hale's warning that rape accusations were easily made and not so easily proven was formalized in American law as preliminary instructions to juries in rape trials until the mid-1970s. At that time the legitimacy of this aged pronouncement (which had been based primarily, it seems, on Hale's authority as a legal expert) was finally questioned, and the jury instruction was struck from U.S. court proceedings. In addition, the practice of imposing the death penalty for rapists (which had been justified by Hale's belief in the particularly heinous nature of rape) was struck down by the Supreme Court in *Coker v. Georgia* in 1972 (No.75-5444).

Despite these changes, the definition of rape as both horrible and easily falsifiable still remains an important locus of discussion about the nature of women and the meaning of rape in the judicial system. Linda Brookover Bourque observes that psychiatric evaluations or lie detector tests are still required to validate victim testimony in many cases (Bourque 1989).

Victims as Liars

Twentieth-century legal writing on the credibility of rape victims went beyond Hale's concerns to differentiate between rape and other crimes. The 1940 edition of the highly respected *Evidence in Trials at Common*

Law, written by legal authority Henry Wigmore, asserted that "no judge should ever let a sex offense charge go to the jury unless the female complainant's social history and mental makeup have been examined and testified to by a qualified physician" (Wigmore 1942, 737). Hale's warning was clearly echoed, but with intensified meaning. Now it was not simply the social circumstances that promoted false accusations of rape but also the actual psychological makeup of female victims. While the character of the woman making the accusation had always been at issue in rape trials, now her character was central and fundamentally questionable.

During the period after 1940, Hale's admonition often took on the character of intensified suspicion toward female complainants found in Wigmore's recommendation. In some essays, the character of any woman charging rape was so questionable that it nearly precluded the possibility of legitimate claims. Authors in law journals set out to establish, and sometimes even assumed, that rape victims were fundamentally untrustworthy. An unsigned 1952 article in the *Yale Law Journal* noted that in a case of rape "the 'facts' may be elusive, ambiguous, and fabricated. And the sexual nature of the crime is conducive to false accusation. Moreover, the word 'rape,' plus the aspect of a 'wronged' girl on the witness stand, may lead to conviction of the defendant, 'though never so innocent'" ("Forcible and Statutory Rape," 1952, 56). Using these basic assumptions as the factual grounding for its claims, this article went on to justify the special treatment of rape cases in trial situations, explaining that

traditionally, American courts have allowed heavy reliance by juries on "demeanor evidence" to gauge credibility. This emphasis reveals a faith in the juror's ability to judge witness truthfulness [based on] appearance on the stand, dress, promptness in answering questions, voice, and attitude. However, the difficulties in determining the truth in rape allegations, coupled with the *unusual inducement to malicious and psychopathic accusation inherent in the sexual nature of the crime,* have led many writers to urge the freer introduction of the findings of psychiatric examinations. (60; emphasis added)

By condemning the female character a priori, legal writers further extended the protections for men accused of rape.

Rape victims were set apart from claimants and witnesses of other felonies both in the introduction of expert psychiatric testimony and in the requirement of corroborating evidence. These concerns and assumptions were echoed in much legal writing until the late 1960s. Sometimes, the fear of false accusation was explicitly voiced, as in an unsigned 1967 monograph in the *Columbia Law Review* which noted, after citing Hale, that "because of the inordinate danger that innocent men will be convicted of rape, some states have adopted the rule that the unsupported testimony of the complaining witness is not sufficient evidence to support a rape conviction" ("Corroborating Charges of Rape," 1967, 1138). Again, these claims were based on fears about the psychology and motivations of women rather than on statistics showing any actual evidence of false convictions in cases of rape. This article continued its argument for special corroborative evidence by observing that

false accusations of sex crimes in general, and rape in particular, are generally believed to be much more frequent than untrue charges of other crimes. A woman may accuse an innocent man of raping her because she is mentally sick or given to delusions; or because, having consented to intercourse, she is ashamed of herself and bitter at her partner; or because she is pregnant, and prefers a false explanation to the true one; or simply because she hates the man whom she accuses. Since stories of rape are frequently lies or fantasies . . . such a story, in itself, should not be enough to convict a man of the crime. (1138)

Significantly, this author, like the author of the *Yale Law Journal* article, argued that the nature of the crime of rape was sufficiently unique to warrant a reevaluation of the role and competence of the jury in cases of rape: "Normally, our law relies on a jury to distinguish truth from falsehood. . . . It is normally assumed, not that false accusations will never occur, but that they will not mislead a jury into convicting. When the crime charged is rape, it is unsafe to rely on this assumption" (1138). In other words, while the normal responsibility of a jury was precisely this adjudication between conflicting stories and determination of falsehood and truthfulness, and although these decisions were normally grounded in examinations of character and credibility of the defendant and witnesses, rape was sufficiently "unique" to require significant alteration in these fundamental legal practices.

Authorities pointed to a high "unfounded" rate in cases of rape as evidence that women did indeed frequently lie about rape. The existence of a high "unfounded" rate for rape, long misunderstood as an index of recanted or false testimony, also underwrote the belief in false accusations. However, the fact that this rate was not carefully scrutinized prior to the mid-1970s is indicative of a tendency to believe evidence that supported the a priori conclusion that women rape claimants were liars. The high unfounded rate for rape was assumed for decades to provide evidence for both the myth of the special nature of rape (because of the ease with which false accusations could be made) and the myth that women tended to fabricate their charges of rape. Because "unfounded" claims were recorded at rates many times higher than that of other felonies, it was thought that women lied much more often than complainants of other crimes.

Scholars in various fields (see Hursch 1977; Taylor 1987) pointed out that while the "unfounded" rate for rape was higher than that of other violent crimes, this had nothing to do with the truth or falsity of the victim's claims. Rather, the "unfounded" rate was a measure of the percentage of cases that were not successfully brought to trial (see Bourque 1989). In fact, the reasons for unfounded rape charges included confused victims' reports to the wrong police jurisdiction, failure of victims to appear in court on assigned dates, and failure of police or medical personnel to adequately gather evidence of whether a rape had been committed or not. In short, the technical term "unfounded" meant anything that did not establish a legitimate case against the rapist. It did not mean that the victim had been proven to be a liar or that she had retracted her claim (see Estrich 1987, chapter 2). Ironically, this statistic could equally have been explained as representing cases dropped by victims with legitimate fears of the trial process. Studies examining reasons for the high rate began to dispel the myth that false accusations of rape were made more often than false accusations of other crimes.

Law reformers have asserted that women are no more likely to lie than victims of other felonies. They have asserted that, given the current state of procedures at hospitals, in police stations, and before and during trials, women were much more likely to fail to report an actual instance of rape than to fabricate a false one. In addition, they argued, the need for corroborative evidence stemming from a presumption of doubt about a victim's claim should be eliminated:

as long as a law in any way indicates that women rape victims shall be trusted less than victims of any other crime, then it's offensive. And it is clearly a statement that the woman witness is not a reliable witness. Such a law predicts how the prosecution will go, it reflects how juries will treat her . . . corroboration is not required in any other crime situation. . . . You don't need corroboration for murder, which is a much more serious offense. (Connell and Wilson 1974, 139)

In many states, the special requirement for corroborative evidence in cases of rape was eliminated. In theory at least, it was possible in those states to obtain a conviction based solely on the victim's word, as was the case for other felonies. Recognizing the justified male fears of false accusation in the face of severe punishments, reformers also argued for a set of graduated offenses as well as for the elimination of the death penalty for rape convictions. A graduated list of offenses was first included in the 1974 Michigan statute.

Consent and Provocation

The questionable believability of rape complainants and the special nature of rape were not the only commonplaces of discussion prior to the 1970s. Other beliefs about the supposed sexual natures of men and women that bolstered the system of traditional thinking about rape included the idea that women "provoked" rape through their dress, actions, or prior reputation. Like the myths already discussed, the idea that women could cause their own rapes did not begin to lose currency until the early 1970s. The publication of Menachim Amir's book-length study, *Patterns in Forcible Rape* (1971), helped unravel this myth.

Amir's 1967 articles, "Victim Precipitated Forcible Rape" (Amir 1967b) and "Forcible Rape" (Amir 1967a), and a chapter of *Patterns in Forcible Rape* grappled with the issue of what he labeled "victim precipitation." "Victim Precipitated Forcible Rape" enumerated the circumstances defining this concept:

the term "victim precipitation" describes those rape situations in which the victim actually, or so it was deemed, agreed to sexual relations but retracted before the actual act or did not react strongly enough when the suggestion was made by the offender(s). The term applies also to cases in risky or vulnerable situations, marred by sexuality, especially when the victim uses what could be interpreted as indecency in language and gestures, or constitute what could be taken as an invitation to sexual relations. (1967b, 495)

Amir's work spelled out how a woman's credibility could be undermined, suggesting that since women know what sorts of situations, actions, and utterances lead to rape, they could and should avoid these behaviors. Amir concluded that "the notion of negligent and reckless behavior on the part of the victim is as important to understanding the offense as is the appearance of these types of behavior in the offender. It does not make any offender innocent, but allows us to consider some of the men, at least, less guilty, and leads us to consider that the victim is perhaps also responsible for what happened to her" (1967b, 502). Without much extrapolation, "reckless behavior on the part of the victim" could become anything that had resulted in rape.

In a second legal monograph, "Forcible Rape," Amir noted that he wished to dispel certain misconceptions with his work, among them that "victims are responsible for their victimization either consciously or by default." Here he added that "the proportion of rapes precipitated by the victim and the characteristics of such acts refute this claim" (1967a, 52). The popular conception that a rape victim gets what she deserves because she is a certain type of person (Amir had linked alcohol use, "meeting in a bar," and "prior bad reputation of victim" to the incidence of victim precipitated rape) was brought into question as Amir grappled with the issue and argued for a new understanding. His 1971 book, regarded as the definitive work on forcible rape up to that point, began to dispel other myths as well, including the idea that almost all rapes occur between strangers. His data showed that more than 13 percent of rapes occurred between close friends, family friends, or relatives, and more than 33 percent occurred between neighbors and acquaintances (1971, 234).

Patterns in Forcible Rape further changed the focus on "victim precipitation." Although the book included a section entitled "Victim-Precipitated Forcible Rape," it emphasized the rapist's misinterpretation of the victim's consent:

the investigator, the law officer, and the court may never know why the offender misconstrues the situation, and they will be completely wrong in considering the victim's behavior and the situation as the "motive for the offense." Asking the offender "why" he interpreted the situation and victim behavior as he did implies that there may be an excuse or a rationalization, while emphasis on vulnerable situations enables the investigator to explain why not all males will resort to rape provided they do not suffer from a certain pathology. (263)

In this work, Amir was interested in establishing the legal relevance of "reckless behavior" and in determining whether this behavior was intentional or not. Amir's language referred to the "victim's contribution to the offense," and concluded that "these results point to the fact that the offender should not be viewed as the sole 'cause' and reason for the offense, and that the 'virtuous' victim is not always the innocent and passive party" (275). The idea that the victim was to blame was retained in modified form.

If women could cause or "precipitate" rape through their dress or behavior, the line between consensual and forced sex was blurred at best. Indeed, legal writers alleged, the adjudication between consent and force in rape cases was one of the most impossible areas for the law: "sometimes the behavior, controlled by personality forces other than those which determine the consciously perceived attitude, will contradict the woman's self-perceived disposition toward the act. When her behavior looks like resistance although her attitude is one of consent, injustice may be done the man by the woman's subsequent accusation" ("Forcible and Statutory Rape" 1952, 66). The ideas underlying this argument are clearly derived from psychoanalytic theory:

the complex set of personality needs, many of them rooted in the unconscious and often competing with each other, may produce an ambivalent and unclear mixture of desire and fear even in the "normal" person . . . the woman's need for sexual satisfaction may lead to the unconscious desire for forceful penetration, the coercion serving neatly to avoid the guilt feelings which might arise after willing participation. But the desire thus generated for the "attack" is likely to clash with the civilized "superego" which vehemently rejects such unrestrained sexuality. ("Forcible and Statutory Rape," 67)

As authors grappled with this problem, they questioned not only the perceptions of the jury or of the accused rapist, but also the ability of the woman herself to know whether she had given consent or not. The suspected pathology of rape victim witnesses suggested not only that they might be outright and deliberate liars, but also that they might actually be uncertain as to whether consent had been given. The supposed female ambivalence toward sex, which leads to presumptions of women's inability adequately to define or certainly to prove consent or lack of consent, is often expressed in the more popular assertion that for women "no means yes." Legal literature suggested, in short, that women did not understand the notion of consent, and so might offer truthful yet inaccurate testimony in court.

The problematic nature of consent and the accompanying notion that at some level women enjoyed rape were reflected in other legal monographs prior to 1970. Between the early fifties and late sixties, the issue of how and when to utilize expert testimony of psychiatrists was frequently discussed. A 1960 article that argued for the use of such expert testimony in four categories of problem cases—those involving "testimony by psychopathic personalities, prosecutions for rape, testimony by drug addicts, and personal injury actions brought by malingerers"—noted (after quoting Hale) that "this type of litigation is especially likely to involve pathological witnesses, the prosecuting witness in particular" (Juviler 1960, 673). This article cites a "prominent psychiatrist" for the information that "most women entertain more or less consciously at one time or another fleeting fantasies or fears that they are being or will be attacked by a man. Of course, the normal woman who has such fantasies does not confuse it with reality but it is . . . easy for some neurotic individuals to translate their fantasies into actual beliefs and memory falsification" (674). The psychiatrist cited, Karl Menninger, is often mentioned in the legal literature for his work with women's rape fantasies. The confusion about what might constitute female nonconsent (since both sincere belief and resistance did not constitute proof) resulted in the requirement that the victim demonstrate "utmost resistance" to obtain a conviction.

Bourque observes that "consent" to rape in the twentieth century sometimes included cases of stranger rape involving "circumstances of force, degradation, brutality, and humiliation," and that "justification for this view included the belief that women were essentially vindictive in nature and that they fantasized and fabricated rapes." Bourque concludes that "whether the result of malicious intent, fear, or confusion, the testimony of rape victims was not considered trustworthy" (Bourque 1989, 98). Attacks on the victim's character, in attempts to "destroy the witness," were made in broad, almost all-encompassing terms. Women who were prostitutes or openly promiscuous had almost no chance of sustaining a rape charge.

Law reformers, however, argued that it was absurd to suppose that women desired rape, and argued instead that rape (especially the question of force versus consent) had little to do with the prior sexual history, manner of dress, or alcohol consumption of the victim. They pointed out that traditional ideas about rape wrongly blamed women for being attacked: "rape is not a price we must pay for our freedom, any more than lynching is the price blacks have to pay for theirs. . . . If we want to place blame anywhere other than on the criminal himself, we must look at the society that creates him. Rape victims have been treated as the guilty ones, the outcasts, for too long" (Medea and Thompson 1974, 5–6). Feminist writers told stories of rapes that illustrated the problem of presumption. Medea and Thompson (1974, 40) relate one story of a woman who resisted: she could have reached a lamp to hit the rapist over the head, but did not do so. The authors note that the rapist thought her failure to use the lamp to resist meant that she wanted to be raped. But when, they asked, according to this way of thinking, should the victim have started to fight? Another writer noted that "most rapes are planned and the victim is usually threatened with death or bodily harm if she resists. Why would a woman go out of her way to be humiliated, to be beaten or possibly killed? The problem with this myth is that it takes the criminal blame away from the rapist and shifts the responsibility for the crime to the victim" (Horos 1974, 12).

Feminists argued that sexual history evidence was clearly irrelevant in cases where the rape was planned, and that rape was a crime of violence rather than sex. Thus, the idea that women "asked for" or secretly desired rape was nonsensical: people do not wish or desire to be violently attacked. This shift was central to the feminist reconceptualization of the crime. Rape law reformers brought new assumptions about male and female sexuality to the law, arguing that males were not likely to lose control at the slightest provocation and that women did not desire forced intercourse.

Consent and Marital Rape

The question of consent also entered the 1970s discussions of rape insofar as it related to the definition of marital rape. Hale was widely quoted on this subject in his assertion that the marriage contract gave consent that could in no way be retracted except through divorce: "a husband cannot be guilty of rape upon his wife for by their mutual matrimonial consent and contract the wife hath given up herself in kind to her husband" ("Marriage, Rape, and the Law," 1978, 22.1). English common law held that rape was "the carnal knowledge of a female, not one's wife, forcibly and against her will" (Bourque 1989, 97). Wives were, in effect, considered part of their husband's property, and rape laws were designed in part to protect husbands (Craik 1984, 177–178).

The idea that wives had already given consent was similar to the rationale used to allow sexual history evidence into court. Both were based on outmoded social situations. The marital rape exemption had been written using the logic that a man's wife belonged to him outright. Even after much sexual history was disallowed, prior sexual relations with the defendant continued to be allowable as relevant to the issue of consent. Feminists worked to remove marital rape exemptions, arguing that even married women deserved the protection of the law and that the marriage contract was not a license to rape.

The Violent Stranger Rapist

Consent was not only related to the victim's character, defined largely as her sexual history, but also to the character of the rapist. The legal tradition defined rapists as evil, lurking strangers, not as law-abiding, hardworking husbands, boyfriends, and fathers. The less familiar a rapist was to his victim and the more random and brutal the attack, the more likely that the law would determine there had been no consent and convict the accused. In the 1970s researchers began to present findings that rape occurred more often between individuals known to each other than between complete strangers (Amir 1971, sec. 13), and research on *marital* rape only emerged a few years later (see Russell 1982).

Closely related to the concept of the "stranger" rapist was the belief, originated and perpetuated in the American South, that most rapes were committed by African-American men against European-American victims who were strangers to them. This resulted in suspicion of both African-American men and African-American female rape claimants.

The charge of rape as a justification for lynching can be traced to the Reconstruction period in the American South. During this era, any sexual relations between European-Americans and African-Americans were illegal, while European-American Southern men could regularly rape African-American women with impunity. African-American men could expect any sexual innuendo toward European-American women to be punished severely.

In addition to keeping European-American and African-American people segregated for the purposes of marriage and reproduction, racist rape ideology provided a ready excuse for lynching. Journalist Ida B. Wells-Barnett worked to show how lynching enforced the social distance between the races during this period (Thompson 1990). Wells-Barnett began the work of documenting the percentage of cases in which rape actually occurred as compared to the percentage in which rape was alleged: "she investigated every lynch case reported to be a consequence of rape. She contended that in every instance the rape story was an invention to gain public sympathy with the lynchers. The cry of rape, she said, was a solution to the problem of some European-American women who were willingly involved with African-American men but were fearful of their reputations" (Thompson 1990, 29). Wells-Barnett showed that under these social and political conditions, a European-American woman might believe she had no alternative to making a false accusation of rape. In the infamous 1932 Scottsboro case in Alabama, African-American adolescents were rounded up and arrested based on the word of European-American teenagers. They were sentenced to life in prison on the basis of little more than their presence at the scene of an alleged rape (see Carter 1969).

Racist justifications for lynching were further explored by Gunnar Myrdal in his 1944 book *An American Dilemma*. Myrdal noted:

the danger of Negroes' desire to rape white women has acquired a special strategic position in the defense of lynching practice. Actually, only 23 percent of the victims were accused of raping or attempting to rape. There is much reason to believe that this figure has been inflated by the fact that a mob which makes the accusation of rape is secure against further investigation; by the broad Southern definition of rape to include all sex relations between Negro men and white women; and by the psychopathic fears of white women in their contacts with Negro men. (Myrdal 1949, 561–562)

In addition, special laws regarding African-American men convicted of rape were in force well into the twentieth century as "courts applied special doctrinal rules to Black defendants accused of the rape or attempted rape of white women . . . [and] the jury was entitled to draw the inference, based on race alone," that the accused African-American man intended to rape the European-American woman (Wriggins 1983, 111). Myrdal's work began to dispel the myth of the African-American rapist (Southern 1987, 79), and this work was advanced by Amir's Philadelphia study, which showed that cases involving African-American rapists and white victims accounted for only 3.3 percent of reported rape cases (Amir 1971, 44).

Significantly, although the doctrinal basis for differential treatment of African-American and European-American rapists was gradually eliminated, statistics on sentencing continued to reveal racial biases. Brownmiller discussed this bias at length, noting that in a study in Baltimore, European-American men accused of raping African-American women received the mildest sentences, while African-American rapists convicted of raping white women received the harshest sentences. Sentences for intraracial rapes averaged between these two types (Brownmiller 1975, 216).

Statistics kept during the late 1950s and early 1960s reflect the easily observed racial identities of accused and accuser: the myth that most rapes involved African-American men attacking European-American women was contradicted by even the earliest statistical information (see Amir 1967). African-American women continued to be treated as illegitimate claimants of rape, as the justice system gave preferential treatment to white victims. Even as a female perspective on rape was validated in legal statutes, it continued to favor the dominant white culture through preferential treatment of European-American defendants and a disproportionate disregard for the word of African-American victims.

When rape was not explained through racist logic, it was often considered a horrific crime perpetrated on unsuspecting strangers by violent, perhaps pathological, sex criminals. There was little recognition that husbands, dates, and other acquaintances from all social classes could be and were rapists. Rapists were consider mentally sick or depraved men who did not display normal social behaviors and personalities. As law reformers challenged other traditional ideas about rape, they also began to research the reasons why men rape and the types of men who rape. They concluded that

our conception of the rapist is often as incorrect and garbled as our conception of his victim. In reality there is no typical rapist just as there is no typical victim. You can't pick him out of a crowd. He looks like other men and, in many ways except one, he is like other men. . . . A disconcerting fact is that rapists appear to be "normal," normal in this sense meaning no different in appearance from society's accepted norm. (Horos 1974, 17)

Increasing evidence on the high incidence of date rape (see Warshaw 1988) and marital rape (see Russell 1982) showed that most rapists were at least acquainted with their victims and that the vast majority of victims were of the same race as their attackers. Additionally, interviews with convicted rapists provided typologies of their reasons for raping. Although these typologies differed on some points, they all recognized the acquaintance or date rapist as well as the more traditionally understood violent stranger rapist (see Beneke 1982; Groth 1979; Sussman and Bordwell 1981).

To summarize, the traditional legal perspective on rape in the United States reflected male fears of false accusation to the point that the word of female victims was almost absolutely mistrusted. The myth that rape was a special crime because of its "sexual nature" and because female claimants were likely to be lying developed in a cultural context in which marriage and chastity were essential to a woman's well-being. In this situation, men feared, the pressures on women discovered in compromising situations were great, and lying about rape presented the best option for saving reputations. The addition of Freudian psychology to the notion that nearly all women claiming to have been raped were fabricating the claim served to support the myth. In turn, this belief underwrote adherence to the idea that consent is difficult to judge, since even the alleged victim might not understand fully if she had granted it. Since the line between force and consent was blurred, the notion that women provoke rape (somewhere between consent and force, as Amir posited), maintained legitimacy. The only "legitimate" claims of rape were those involving either violent stranger rapists and strong corroborative evidence (such as eye-witness testimony), and those involving European-American claimants and racially marginalized defendants. The law did not reflect the experiences of female victims of rape.

The Rape Law Reform Response

Starting in the early 1970s, rape law reformers sought to replace traditional myths about rape with a revised set of beliefs which, taken together, constituted an alternative understanding of the nature of female victims, male rapists, and the crime of rape. These reformers had observed the alarmingly low rate of convictions in rape trials and the development of trial practices that had become known as the "second rape." They set out both to increase the number of successful convictions and to improve the trial experiences of female victims.

The traditional legal view of rape represented an interlocking system of beliefs. The belief that women were likely to lie was integrally related to the notion that rape was a special crime. In turn, the belief that women were unclear, even in their own minds, about whether they had consented to intercourse was closely connected with the idea that most rape victims were liars. Reformers thus offered a comprehensive set of counter-proposals about the causes of rape and how it could best be treated under the law. To achieve their goals of less brutal trial experiences for victims and higher conviction rates for perpetrators, reformers had to bring rape law up to date with contemporary social reality.

The reformers' efforts centered on the assertions that the crime of rape could be adjudicated by a jury just as other felonies were; that because women were not pathological liars and their social roles had changed, the incentives to invent a fictional rape were much less significant than the incentives to conceal that it had occurred; and that women did not cause rape through their behavior, dress, attitudes, or reputations. They argued that the same rules used to judge the credibility of witnesses of other felonies could be used in rape cases. They also argued that rapists could not be identified by their race or class affiliations but by the testimony of their victims, that rapists were not necessarily strangers to their victims, and that rape was a crime of violence. In short, reformers offered a coherent set of beliefs that directly contradicted and were intended to replace traditional views.

Perhaps the clear connections between social and judicial concepts about rape have made the law reform effort an especially ambitious one. Fueled by male fears and concerns, one set of beliefs had developed into a coherent mindset about rape that was difficult to refute. Likewise, it is only as a coherent and fully articulated set of ideas that the reform views can make sense as a rational alternative. This mutually reinforcing characteristic of the individual beliefs that make up rape ideology offers an opportunity for popular discourses to contain and limit new meanings: by fragmenting discussions of rape law reform and thereby suppressing the complete alternative belief system, popular discourses have at times rendered the overall project incoherent or ill-conceived. Although some aspects of the reform conception have been accepted into mainstream understanding, the logical structure of reformist belief has not: reformist logic, it seems, has seldom been presented to a mass audience. This fragmented representation of rape law reform in mainstream news and fictionalized narratives will be examined in Chapters 4 and 5.

Although the two mutually exclusive belief systems about rape have coexisted for at least two decades, the inclusion of reformed ideas in mass-mediated treatments of rape has been fragmentary and slow. The following chapter discusses the significance of trials in mainstream national discussions of rape. The cases under examination here each provided an opportunity for mainstream ideology to assert a position in relation to reform ideology, and each case illustrates the response of the dominant discourse to this concerted effort at change.

Chapter 3
Issue-Oriented Trials in the Context of Social Change

Highly publicized trials have become a staple of American news coverage in recent years. The cases of Mike Tyson, Matthew Stuart, O. J. Simpson, and the Los Angeles police officers accused of brutally beating Rodney King are among the profusion of cases that have received prolonged national news attention. Beyond a few common elements such as emotional drama, sex, betrayal, and violence, what do these trials have in common and why are they such an omnipresent element of our mainstream news? Although such cases have become so common that there is nearly always a trial underway in the national spotlight, this is by no means a new phenomenon. Indeed, scholarship on the political trial reflects a long tradition of public cases in the United States (see Christenson 1986; Belknap 1981). Public trials have long been used to delineate right from wrong, good from evil, acceptable from unacceptable, and political activists have chosen trials as forums for articulating and publicizing their points of view.

Recent work on political trials suggests that at present they are more likely to be related to the "issues of the day" than to particular political agendas of the parties involved in the case. According to Belknap: "In the United States, political trials usually have occurred at times when the status quo was under serious challenge, generally during periods of social and political ferment" (1981, 14). He concludes that "one may properly apply the term 'political trial' to any trial or impeachment that immediately affects or is intended to affect the structure, personnel, or policies of government, that is the product of or has its outcome determined by political controversy, or that results from the efforts of a group within society having control of the machinery of government to disadvantage its rivals in a power struggle" (6). As Christenson notes, certain trials function to "bring together for public consideration society's basic contradictions, through an examination of competing values and loyalties" (1986, 3). This is certainly true of highly publicized rape trials, which are seldom selected as "test cases" by reformers (thus limiting their potential to illustrate some point of law), but rather become well known primarily because of their subject matter.

Increasingly, our news is filled with stories of trials involving current social issues: hate crime, sexual harassment and assault, police brutality, and "political correctness" have all been explored in high-profile cases. These trials are at center related to social change movements that have been successful in bringing their concerns into the national spotlight. This proliferation of trials that do not fit old frameworks has led to a discussion of the changing nature and possible functions of public trials (Schuetz and Snedaker 1988; Hariman 1990). Hariman argues for a genre called the "popular trial" that encompasses political trials and others, but does not specify the types that comprise this general category. In this chapter I divide into three easily recognizable types a number of highly publicized trials that have previously been the subject of scholarly attention. I then argue for the existence and importance of the issue-oriented trial as a fourth type, represented by the Rideout, Big Dan's, and Dotson cases. This subgenre is essential to our understanding of social movements and their effectiveness: the trials serve important functions in the playing out of social issues in mainstream culture. The specific issues that brought each of these three trials to national attention are previewed at the end of this chapter.

A Typology of Highly Publicized Trials

Highly publicized trials involve widely divergent issues and defendants. If we are to understand the differences between, for example, the Julius and Ethel Rosenberg trial and the William Kennedy Smith trial, we must begin by defining a clear typology for public trials. Both trials were about the power to define right and wrong and the power to punish or acquit, and both can usefully be studied as places where these definitions and powers were enacted. Yet one involved alleged traitors during wartime, and the other implicated a member of a prominent family for a crime irrelevant to the national security. What significant elements distinguish these trials from each other? What links them together as part of a common cultural phenomenon? Determining a typology is a first step toward gaining a more sophisticated understanding of how these trials function and why they cover such a wide range of issues.

Often, typologies are offered to be discussed and eventually refined or even replaced; no doubt the following typology, too, will be refined and developed. The following categories do not exist as completely distinct units such that every public trial fits neatly into one category or the other. Still, although some cases have become highly publicized for more than one of the reasons outlined below, the categories are nonetheless sufficiently distinct to warrant separate scholarly attention.

A review of the cases that have been discussed by scholars of popular and political trials suggests that previously studied publicized trials fit into three general categories. First, many of these trials serve to highlight a particular legal issue or involve a crime committed deliberately by parties wishing to call attention to their point of view or cause. The trials of the Catonsville Nine, convicted and sent to prison for burning draft records with napalm (Hariman 1990), and of Leona Benten, recently arrested for bringing the contraceptive RU486 into the country (Lewin 1992), are two examples. In each case, the defendants were part of a larger social movement with a broad agenda for social change, and each deliberately committed a crime in order to call attention to the injustice they sought to eradicate. Many Supreme Court cases, such as *Roe v. Wade*, belong in this category.[1] They are chosen by attorneys, by the court, or by parties to the case as particularly well suited to the task of illustrating a legal issue or position. This category includes trials for crimes directly related to the political or legal point being advanced by the defendant(s), but also includes trials for which the crime is merely a means of obtaining a forum for a political or legal point of view (such as trespassing trials at which the defendants read into the court record their opposition to nuclear power).

These trials can best be studied as *movement strategy*, and both scholars and activists can learn from an analysis of elements that contribute to the successes and failures of such strategies. This type of trial can also be studied for insights into how the challenged group or ideology responds rhetorically to the strategy for gaining public attention and political power. Studies of this category of trial would look at the successes (national attention, or legal action) achieved by the "deliberate" criminal, as well as when and how this strategy is most likely to achieve success. Is this a desperation strategy for tiny and powerless groups, or is it shared by larger and better developed movements? Is it used to gain attention for an issue in such a way that immediate action or change is likely? What do movement representatives have to do to get national attention and what kind of attention does this strategy yield? What kinds of arguments accompany this strategy? These are important questions to ask in trying to understand the deliberate dialogue that takes place between movement strategists and establishment forces in such trials.

In some cases, the actions of a group, because of its agenda, are viewed by the dominant culture as a threat to national interests. Thus, to some degree many of these trials overlap with the second category of trials that regularly seem to receive public attention and scholarly analysis. These trials involve matters of obvious or arguable national significance: the crime is assumed to be of interest to the general public because of its relevance to national identity, security, or stability. Trials that have been considered "political" trials in scholarly literature are of this type. The category includes trials of traitors, spies, communists, anarchists, terrorists, and assassins. Famous trials in this category include the Chicago Haymarket trial and the trials of Angela Davis, John Hinckley, Julius and Ethel Rosenberg, Sacco and Vanzetti, and the Chicago Seven. All gained national importance because of the perceived threat to national interests posed by the defendants. These trials can be usefully studied in order to gain insights into where, when, how, and why dominant political forces have felt threatened and how they have marshalled arguments in defense of the status quo. In general, these cases were selected for attention by a dominant group in an overt attempt to set the parameters for what is acceptable and unacceptable in the political realm.

This type of trial can best be studied not as movement strategy but as the political strategy of the empowered representatives of government and law, since the representatives of the dominant culture chose the criminals and crimes through which to illustrate both their power and their definitions of right, wrong, truth, and falsehood. Scholars of these trials should ask why particular cases came to the national attention and what perceived threat was being resisted through publicity in a particular case. They should ask whether the strategy of selecting and publicizing a case in a particular way was useful to the maintenance of power or to the maintenance of a given understanding of truth or morality. Finally, scholars should examine whether and to what extent dissident voices were heard in the process of the publicity surrounding these trials. Do some of these trials provide the ground for expressing and defining a national identity for which there is no dissident voice? (For example, there is seldom a publicly articulated argument that an assassin was right to shoot the president.)

Many of these cases, such as the Haymarket trial, have in retrospect become examples of errors in justice, a phenomenon equally worthy of scholarly attention. The progression from the point of public statement of parameters to the point where the case has become an embarrassment or example of judicial error offers fertile ground for the study of ideological change of a different sort than that under examination here. What makes hegemonic forces enact these egregious examples of "justice"? Are they threatened enough that the risk of appearing arbitrary or ruthless must be taken? Under what circumstances does this happen, and with what results? What are the conditions under which a culture comes to realize an "error" in justice and label it as such?

Finally, a third category of public trial can be identified as celebrity cases, or cases that are given media attention primarily because of the high-profile identity of the parties involved: trials of individuals like Claus von Bulow, O. J. Simpson, Mike Tyson, and Bruno Richard Hauptman receive widespread attention because either the defendant or the plaintiff has achieved national prominence before the trial. These trials are less about power and definitions of truth and morality than about entertainment. These trials should be studied primarily as an entertainment genre through which viewers and readers gain knowledge about celebrities and their lifestyles and secondarily as public discussions of contemporary issues and morality. Scholars of trials in this group should determine the extent to which the coverage is about personality and the extent to which it is about a salient contemporary issue or struggle. The amount and focus of media attention given to celebrity cases should be compared with that afforded non-celebrity cases. While some discussions in mainstream news will certainly involve the central issues of the case, much of it will also focus on the identity of the celebrity and her or his previous activities and lifestyle, and much of the meaning-making of the news will take place in the context of these personal factors. Clearly, a case may involve a celebrity and also fit into one of the other two categories discussed above.

These three categories represent the primary factors fuelling national publicity in cases that have *to this point* received scholarly attention. However, although some rape trials are also celebrity trials (such as the William Kennedy-Smith and the Mike Tyson trials), the three cases studied here were not celebrity or movement strategy cases, nor were they concerned with national identity or security. The Rideout, Big Dan's, and Dotson cases fit into a new genre of highly publicized trial that I call the "issue-oriented" trial. Issue-oriented trials should be considered separate at the outset because the primary reasons for their publicity are different from those of the trials that have been studied in the past, and they fit none of the defining criteria outlined above.

These trials would not be considered part of the feminist movement according to traditional social movement scholarship: the trials themselves do not represent feminist agitation or strategy, but rather are an indirect result of it. While feminists were responsible for placing rape and our understanding of it on the national agenda through rape law reform, they had no discernable voice either in selecting these trials as vehicles for examination of the issues or in selecting the terms in which the trials would be discussed, carried out, or interpreted in nationally available media.

At the same time, this very publicity has served to place feminist ideas about rape on the national agenda. The publicity afforded these trials, both in news and in fiction, has unquestionably been an important part of the public adjudication between opposing realities of rape. Rape law reformers argued for the validity of their nontraditional understanding of rape but had little control over when and how their conception of rape would be dispersed. Similar phenomena mark the selection and discussion of trials on issues other than rape.

The Rodney King case is perhaps one of the most widely publicized examples of an issue-oriented trial, yet in the past decade other trials have gained similar national attention. Many of these cases reflect specific issues that were brought to the fore by social movements, while others involve issues of cultural politics that pit one subcultural group against another and are indirectly related to social change: the Bensonhurst case centered on white teenagers in Brooklyn, New York, who beat a black youth to death after he entered a predominantly white neighborhood to buy a car; the McDuffy case in Liberty City, Florida, implicated white police officers for police brutality against a black man, but they were acquitted by an all-white jury; and the Los Angeles case of Soon Ja Du involved a Korean grocery store clerk who shot black teenager Latasha Harlins in the back of the head (Mydans 1992). Each of these cases focused on contemporary social issues that have become salient because of social movements or social change. News coverage of these cases enacted the acceptance and rejection of new ideas and claims against the dominant ideology. As with the subject of rape, public trials offer one of the primary occasions for national discussion of these significant contemporary issues.

An issue-oriented trial is publicized because a movement for social change has placed a particular topic on the national agenda or because social change has produced a new concern. Even the publicity surrounding the McMartin preschool trial (1990) resulted from a social movement that has fought for the recognition of children's abuse by trusted caregivers and for the legitimacy of children's stories of such abuse. The McMartin case provided the ground on which arguments for and against the legitimacy of child testimony in court could be articulated before a national audience. Likewise, it took place within the context of a rapid increase in the proportion of mothers working outside the home, the accompanying crisis in finding day care, and parental fears about adequate supervision. Such a case simply would not have reached the national news media in an era unmarked by such changes. These cases, however, are often not well suited to illustrating the issues and questions at hand: these trials do not illustrate points but rather provide for a public discussion of crucial contemporary issues.

The stature of some rape trials in popular media is clearly traceable to the inroads already made by feminist discourses into mainstream thought and political agendas since the 1970s; these trials are newsworthy because of the high visibility of gender politics in the ensuing years. Rape law reformers have gained widespread attention by questioning the process of the rape trial; in turn, specific trials have been selected— *though not by movement strategists*—as forums for explicating or "hashing out" the conflicting perspectives. In the discourse surrounding these public trials, traditional ideas often have given way to oppositional ways of understanding complex issues of truth, character, innocence, and guilt. The issue-oriented trial is political primarily because of its subject matter and/or its socio-political context, independent of the identity or intentions of any of the parties involved. The recent successes of social movements in placing their issues on the national agenda have in effect forced the national media to publicize trials on those same subjects, as can be seen in the Rideout, Big Dan's, and Dotson cases.

The Cultural Significance of Issue-Oriented Trials

The genre of issue-oriented trials exists because it fulfills a function in the process of social change. The media attention afforded some cases will always be justifiable (and overtly justified): incredible brutality, personality quirks, and social marginality are all grist for wide media exposure. Although the facts of a case may appear to be sufficiently important to justify national attention, the peculiarities of individual cases introduce an element of chance (or remove the element of absolute control) into the processes of social change and the formation of public opinion. But giving attention only to case-specific details misses the larger and more important point: national coverage of issue-oriented trials offers an opportunity for the whole culture to come to a decision about how much change and what specific elements of change are acceptable at a given time and on a particular issue.

These types of trials are selected for prolonged national news coverage for two primary reasons. First, they offer an opportunity for mainstream discourse to take up the issues for which social change movements have demanded public attention: the process of adjudication whereby some ideas are coopted and validated as a part of the mainstream while others are rejected or ignored is taken up in media discussions of these issue-oriented cases. Second, the discussion of these trials is played out as a nationally visible power struggle on an issue where the criteria for innocence and guilt are known to be in flux. On a nationwide level, readers and observers witness how power is wielded in a system of changing values and definitions. Both the trial itself and the news coverage that accompanies it are evidence of social change in progress.

Cases involving issues of social change gain notoriety in the context of a social movement that has placed particular issues at the forefront of our national agenda. National news coverage of these cases serves as an illustration of how power is currently being wielded by the powerful in the face of claims of injustice by the less empowered. Will the existing power structure alter its decision-making procedures or its definitions of innocence and guilt in the given case? Or will it put off this change until a future case brings the same issue back into the national spotlight? Through these highly publicized cases, we witness the struggle for control over the way change will be undertaken and the struggle over the limits of that change. The structures and values of news and fiction contribute greatly to the enactment of this process, as Chapters 4 and 5 will show.

National news coverage of these cases is more important and more complex than a simple witnessing of whether or not the verdict will favor a challenging ideology on a contemporary social issue. Mainstream news discourse can serve as a public record of more subtle shifts in mainstream thought. Even if the verdict does not favor the challenger, news discourse may nonetheless show that a more subtle, yet still significant, ideological shift has taken place. The specific law reform issues central to the three cases under examination are outlined below.

Central Issues of Social Change in the Rideout, Big Dan's, and Dotson Cases

The three cases examined here did not break new legal ground. At first glance, the Rideout case may seem to have importance as a test case for the new Oregon marital rape law. However, *Rideout* did not have the required specifications of a good test case: although it did enjoy the status of a legal "first" (since Rideout was the first man to be tried for raping his wife while living with her), many expert commentators noted that no matter what the outcome, it could not make or break the new law. The one law review essay on the case noted that "although the case was a first, assiduously watched by members of women's liberation groups throughout the nation, it was by no means a milestone . . . some unsettled legal considerations were left dangling which will have to wait another day, another case" (Schiff 1979, 55–56). *Rideout* could not really test the new law because the central legal issue was whether a man could be convicted of raping his own wife. Only a conviction would signal the *validity* of the new law. Likewise, establishing *lack of validity* would have required that an acquittal be predicated on the parties' marital status: that is, on whether, if the parties involved had *not* been married to each other, the case would have resulted in a conviction. Even if the Rideouts had not been husband and wife, the volume and variety of character

evidence brought against Greta Rideout, and the lack of significant corroborating testimony or evidence, would have made this a complicated
case. As a consequence, John Rideout's acquittal did not signal that the
new law was invalid, nor did the case serve as a "test."

Apart from this legal technicality, it is possible that one reason the
Rideout case gained prolonged national attention was its status as a
national "first." Yet this is the most substantial claim to legal importance
that can be made for any of these three cases, which kept the issue of
rape in the national spotlight almost continually from 1978 to 1986: of
the three cases under discussion here, only *Rideout* has even this much
legal significance. And these three cases were the subject of a total of
only five law review articles, all of which focused on media attention. It
is likely that these cases would have received no attention in law journals had they not first been highly publicized. If these rape cases were
not legally important, then what accounts for the abundant national
mainstream media attention afforded them?

The Rideout Case: What Is "Marital Rape?"

Since Oregon had eliminated its marital rape exemption at the time of
the Rideout case (thus becoming one of three states in which it was
illegal for a husband to rape his wife while living with her), the central
issue of the trial was the validity of the new law. Beyond this, the case
also highlighted the terms in which the new law could be understood
and utilized.

John Rideout's attorney Charles Burt summarized the history of the
idea of "prior consent" as follows:

the rule [of prior consent] was first recognized in the United States [in 1857]. . . .
It has been the rule all through the history of this country and the rule in every
state. The marriage contract includes a consent to sexual relations which can
not be withdrawn, except by a decree of the Court dissolving the marriage and
terminating the contract. People enter into marriage with this agreement and
the State cannot change their agreement by changing the laws. ("Memorandum
of Law—Demurrer," 1)

In *Rideout*, the judge rejected Burt's argument that the new law was
not legally binding. This served to shift the dispute over consent away
from "prior consent" and into the realm of corroborating evidence of
"forcible compulsion."

In legal terms, the special nature of marital rape extended even beyond that of nonmarital rape with regard to the alleged ease and frequency with which false charges could be brought. Since it had been
a legal impossibility for so long, marital rape was not seen as particu-

larly horrific, but it *was* seen as a particularly difficult area for legal intervention. Defense attorney Burt argued that the marital relation was an inappropriate realm for law since it would be too difficult to regulate the details of marital intimacy. Since consent would presumably be more difficult to adjudicate, false claims of rape would be easier to make within marriage. A California assemblyman noted that rape was difficult to prosecute and that marital rape would be even more difficult ("Case for a Spousal-Rape Law," 1979). If marital rape were admitted as a possibility, the potential difficulties in discovering truth would be even greater than those in nonmarital rape cases because of the history of previous consent to intercourse between the parties. As the first laws allowing for marital rape emerged, many legal commentators seemed at a loss to imagine how such a rape might be satisfactorily proven. Thus a good test case would have to be unquestionably clear in all other respects (use of force, lack of consent, and unimpeachable character of the victim). In retrospect, one author noted, "the reluctance to punish spousal rape with penalties commensurate with other types of rape showed the continuing uncertainty that rape was, in law, even possible between husband and wife" (Kivett 1986, 1047). If consent, compulsion, and corroboration were viewed as legally problematic areas in nonmarital rape, they could only be perceived as more problematic in cases of marital rape.

In his defense of John Rideout, Burt sought to capitalize on this lack of specificity on the question of proof, characterizing the Rideout marriage as one filled with arguments followed by "kiss-and-make-up" episodes. Burt argued that "if the Defendant honestly believed he had a right, by virtue of his marriage contract, to engage in sexual intercourse without the consent of his wife, and was acting in this state of mind, he would not have . . . criminal intent" ("Defendant's Requested Jury Instructions," #6). Using this logic, John Rideout would be considered innocent because he held traditional values and beliefs with respect to marriage. Thus, the Rideout case centered on the issues of whether marital rape was a legitimate crime and, beyond that, how such a crime could be defined in order to effectively implement the law. John Rideout was acquitted in part because his case was the first of its kind and he was, in a sense, caught between two systems of law and morality. He could not have been convicted of rape because he held traditional views, so the traditional proofs would have had to have been overwhelming to demonstrate his guilt.

The Big Dan's Case: Victim Character, Provocation, and Consent

The central reform issues in this case were the definition of consent and the relevance of the victim's character to the question of whether or not she had been raped. Reluctant eye-witness testimony corroborating the victim's story was also central to the prosecution's argument, and although rape law reformers had fought for the acceptance of uncorroborated victim testimony, the case did not illustrate progress on this issue, nor did it offer a counter-example to the stranger-rapist myth.

Defense attorneys in the Big Dan's case utilized the traditional methods for attacking the victim's credibility, accusing her of "cheating on welfare" while "living with" the father of her children. In addition, the defense suggested that the victim was a psychologically unstable person who had been under psychiatric care at the time of the alleged rape, and they also attempted to connect the victim with a previous "recanted" charge of rape. They hoped to damage the victim's general character and suggest that, as a person of low credibility, she might be lying about the rape.

Because of the traditional way in which rape trials had been conducted, and because it had proven successful in the past, the defense attorneys chose a consent defense as a second line of argument in this case. They hoped to prove that the woman had encouraged the men to have intercourse with her and had later decided to label this activity a rape. The prosecution defended the witness's credibility by suggesting that the idea of consenting to the activities described was implausible:

Let us look on the question of consent first of all to impartial evidence. . . . Let's look at the evidence provided first of all from Robert Silva, from Daniel O'Neil, from Michael O'Neil, who know none of these parties, who do not know these defendants, nor do they know [the victim]; they have no bias. And when we think of consent, when we think of how long it went on, and what went on, we must think of the character of the woman who enjoyed and desired and wanted it. You saw her with your own eyes, you could look at her, you could hear her. Did she have dignity? Did she have dignity?" ("Commonwealth vs. Joseph Vieira and Commonwealth vs. Daniel C. Silva," 10)

The prosecution's closing statement, with its direct reference to the myth of consent in rape, demonstrated eloquently the degree to which this was an easy case to adjudicate—even with respect to old understandings of rape. This statement was an expression of why a victim was not likely to lie about rape, but would instead more likely fail to report it. Prosecutor Veary also argued that the victim was particularly valiant in her efforts to work against "the myth":

[The victim] is going to have a hard time explaining that she may have been at that bar having a couple of drinks. She knows the costs of that. She knows the costs of that in terms of the myth. And that's why, I suggest to you, there are certain exaggerations and inconsistencies in those early stories. I'm not talking fear, necessarily, and I'm not talking hysteria, I'm talking myth. And the effort to try to down that myth, the effort of one young woman to work against that myth. She knows how people treat rape victims. And in her mind, I suggest to you, the only way of battling against that was to build some sort of fortress around her; to perhaps exaggerate a point here, exaggerate a point there, but I would remind you once again: Think about this case at the door of Big Dan's tavern; that woman running out, naked from the waist down, with those injuries, screaming. ("Commonwealth vs. Joseph Vieira and Commonwealth vs. Daniel C. Silva," 17–87)

Thus, salient law reform issues in this case were the victim's character and general veracity and the question of whether women desire or give consent to rape.

The Dotson Case: Victim Credibility and Ease of False Accusation

When Cathleen Crowell Webb came forward with her public recantation of the 1979 testimony that had sent Gary Dotson to prison, the reform issues during the resulting hearings centered on two issues: victim credibility (was Webb lying in 1979 or in 1985?) and the degree of ease with which a false accusation of rape could be made (could Webb have fooled everyone in making a false claim of rape?). This second issue again raised the question of the special nature of the crime of rape, this time with regard to the ability of juries to judge witnesses' credibility. These issues received significant attention in law review discussions subsequent to the 1985 hearings.

During the 1979 trial, characterizations of both Webb and Dotson followed the long-held notions of "appropriate" rapist and victim. Dotson's attorney complained vociferously about the prosecution's language that characterized Dotson as "burned out" and Cathleen Crowell as a "sixteen-year-old virgin." Webb at the time of the original trial was portrayed as an "acceptable" rape victim. The trial received no national media coverage and little local coverage. Similarly, the 1985 recantation was not particularly significant or noteworthy from a legal perspective. Law review essays focused on the presentation of the legal perspective on the case, in contrast to the portrayal that had been produced by mainstream news coverage.

At the time of Dotson's conviction in 1979, the legal burden of proof had shifted to the point that he was considered guilty until proven innocent. The legal discourse on *Dotson* in 1985 focused on this point, emphasizing repeatedly that confidence in the legal system was based on the presumption of accurate judgment in the original trial. In addition, legal discourse routinely included the assertion that recanted testimony was always viewed with suspicion. Since Webb's credibility had been favorably evaluated in 1979, the legal position on her recantation was one of suspicion and doubt:

recanting testimony is regarded as very unreliable, and a court will usually deny a new trial based on that ground where it is not satisfied that such testimony is true. . . . The affidavit of a recanting witness is not entitled to so much weight as to justify the conclusion that the evidence given by him was corrupt and willfully false. The conclusion of the jury would rather warrant the presumption that his testimony was truthful and his affidavit false. (516 N.E. 2nd 718, Ill. App. 1 Dist. 1987)

The rejection of her recanted story was defended based on the idea that "Webb's retraction of her identification of Dotson is not persuasive. . . . Webb's purported motive in charging rape, her fear of pregnancy, also undercuts her story" (Taylor 1987, 68). Observers in legal journals asserted that the jury system was capable of handling rape cases just as it did any other case, and that Webb's demeanor on the night of the rape had been consistent with that of a rape victim, characterized by her "extreme conduct on the night of the assault—her shuddering, hysteria, and fear of men" (Frossard 1988, 15).

The crucial issue, however, was Webb's veracity in recanting, and her new story was discounted because "she picked the most implausible story for a recantation . . .[there are] several other forms of recantation that might be more plausible. . . . She could say she identified the wrong man. . . . Or say it was some sort of a consensual act" (Black 1985, 59). Webb's manner during the 1985 clemency hearing was not consistent with her professed truthfulness, since she was "evasive, combative, and prone to selective memory" (Black 1985, 58). Webb had been extremely credible on the night of the rape and at the subsequent trial: "all her conduct [in 1977] was consistent with that of a rape victim—hysteria, crying, scared, bruised, battered, torn clothing, signs of trauma, scratches on the abdomen. And she gave a very prompt, believable complaint of rape the minute she got to the police station that convinced police officers, emergency room doctors, and even parents" (Black 1985, 59). Her 1985 recantation was less believable. Judge Richard Samuels summed up the difference between Webb at the original trial and at the clemency hearing: "demeanor is one of the factors that determines credibility. In 1979, at the trial, she was very forthright, not a bit evasive. Very candid. Her demeanor was that of a person actually telling a true story—and she was unshaken on rigorous cross-examination. In April [1985] she was evasive throughout" (Black 1985, 59). Legal commentators generally concluded that "her memory had lapsed too often for her to be credible" (Frossard 1988, 59).

If Webb had chosen a different story, one consistent with the physical evidence, she could have cleared Dotson in a legally valid way, either in 1977, before the original trial, or in 1985, with her choice of recantation: "If Dotson had not raped her, Webb could merely have said in 1977 that she didn't see the rapist in the police photographs" (Taylor 1987, 68). Relevant issues, then, were her veracity in 1977–79 and 1985, and the criteria used to judge witnesses' credibility.

Fictionalized Portrayals of Highly Publicized Trials

Each of these three cases brought one or two central reform issues into the national spotlight by providing a specific ground for adjudication between selected traditional ideas about rape and the reformed alternative. Each of these issues received significant attention in mainstream news coverage of the relevant case, although coverage was by no means limited to these issues.

In addition to bringing contested issues into the national discourse through news coverage, many of the issue-oriented cases in recent years have become the subjects of books, television movies-of-the-week, or Hollywood films. This phenomenon further indicates that what is truly important about these cases is that they provide specific subjects for the adjudication of social change in the public realm. All three of the cases under discussion became the subject of fictionalized re-presentations subsequent to the completion of the trial. Although the forms they took differed (two television movies-of-the-week, one Hollywood film, and one autobiographical book), all three clearly advanced the public discourse surrounding both the specific cases and the issues they brought to national attention. The retelling of these case histories indicates, at the least, that the trial is not the end of the story. In a broader context, fictionalized portrayals can be seen as an additional step in the process of accommodation that is always taking place between the dominant ideology and the social movements that challenge its precepts, assumptions, and myths. Fictionalized portrayals of these cases brought a sharper focus to relevant reform issues.

The re-presentation of real-life cases has become a staple of the American entertainment industry. Often, these retellings deal with an issue-oriented trial, and often they incorporate and articulate the arguments on at least two sides of a difficult contemporary issue or subject. These retellings, then, offer a second terrain on which the struggle for meaning and legitimacy is fought. Not only do these texts represent a second stage in the adjudication process, but they also represent a more articulate and detailed discussion of the salient issues. The two chapters that follow provide the details of how this process of change has been accomplished in news coverage and fictionalized re-presentations.

Note

1. Over the past fifteen years, there have been no Supreme Court cases among the many nationally publicized trials that dealt with rape. Because rape laws are decided by individual states, highly publicized rape trials have been state cases that were covered by the national news media. Some Supreme Court cases on other issues have been highly publicized: Celeste Condit's book *Decoding Abortion Rhetoric: Communicating Social Change* (Chicago: University of Chicago Press, 1990), discusses the significant relationship between public discourse and the *Roe v. Wade* decision.

Chapter 4
Mainstream Coverage: Trials as News Events

Given the values and objectives that define news in the United States, it is not surprising that so many news stories about social problems and issues turn on courtroom drama: trials offer vivid conflicts between opposing sides of a dispute, and they also offer easy access to "experts" who serve as sources of information and opinion.

An important goal of news media is to be popular (Schuetz and Snedaker 1988; Fiske 1989), but the conventions of popular news invariably constrain its content (see van Dijk 1988; Bennett 1988; Altschull 1984). Reporters and analysts highlight personal and dramatic details in a given story, yet they "almost always retreat from opportunities to explain the power structures and political processes that lie behind the issues" (Bennett 1988, 23). A narrow focus on dramatic personal information is accompanied by a reluctance to cover any subject in depth (by way of extended discussion and explanation, placement of the issue in context, or explanation of technicalities of logic or procedure). Rape trials fit the criteria for popular news coverage that ensure their continued selection as news events. Conversely, other potential news events, such as the opening of a national rape crisis line or changes in legislation, do not readily fit the criteria for popular news and receive much less media attention.

Conventional news values affect the coverage of trials in ways that hinder the expression of new voices, in this case, the voices of law reformers and the victims they support. However, standard journalistic practices and values may also allow for the expression and legitimation of selected elements of the victim's experience. Trials involve a series of unfolding events and testimony that is easily portrayed as a dramatic narrative featuring conflict between two parties, drawing attention and focus away from larger and potentially confusing or complicated issues. Indeed, reporters are advised "against becoming involved with legal issues and developments of the trial" (Schuetz and Snedaker 1988, 9).

News media also rely on quotes from "expert" sources and people personally involved with the case to establish the credibility of a story. Van Dijk (1988) includes among the "special means to enhance . . . [the] appearance of truth and plausibility" of news discourse the criteria of "using evidence from sources, especially when opinions are involved" and "using evidence from other reliable sources (authorities, respectable people, professionals)" (84).

Although other conventions affect the construction of news coverage in the United States, the use of drama, personal details, and expert commentary have the most relevance to the coverage of trials because they represent the central appeal of trials for news organizations. These characteristics are largely responsible for the fact that so much news surrounding contemporary issues focuses on specific trials, and they also affect the content of trial coverage.

Containment of Rape Reform Ideas in Mainstream News

News coverage, though purporting and attempting to be "objective," presents a skewed picture of many trials, emphasizing verbatim testimony related to character that can be attention-getting, colorful, and even shocking. In rape trials, with their traditional emphasis on the credibility of the victim (who is the key witness to the crime) and their ban on evidence concerning the defendant's sexual history, coverage of the proceedings disproportionately focuses on the character and credibility of the victim, just as in the trial itself. Recently, the elimination of victims' sexual history evidence from trials in accordance with "rape shield" laws has in turn reduced the centrality of such discussion in news reports. In the Rideout trial, where this evidence was allowed, the preponderance of damaging personal information about Greta Rideout suggested a verdict of "not guilty" for John even at the very beginning of the trial. During the Big Dan's trial, where sexual history evidence regarding the victim was barred, news coverage was more sympathetic to the victim.

Since descriptions of systems of logic, reasoning, or action are not considered newsworthy, there has been a notable absence of discussion about the rape law reform movement in news coverage of these trials. The reluctance to explain the legal reasoning behind either the defense or prosecution arguments has resulted in the reporting of testimony out of context, without enough detail to be understood or interpreted. The reporting in these cases followed a familiar pattern: neither the traditional legal stance on rape nor the reformed view were described as unified perspectives on rape law that stood in contrast to each other. This has disadvantaged the reform position, which is far behind the traditional view in terms of its dispersal and acceptance among the public. Most people reading about rape trials in the newspaper or watching coverage on television know little about the feminist alternative to mainstream ideas about rape. This was especially true in the early stages of the rape law reform movement. Since coverage of both views has been fragmented and overdramatized, readers and viewers have not easily learned the logic of the reform perspective.

The fragmented nature of news thus advantages the better known traditional view, although it appears to be neutral or unbiased. Neither understanding of rape is well articulated in news discourse, but the sense-making framework of coverage has been derived from traditional myths. The focus on personalized issues, in fact, has often implicitly reinforced traditional notions about rape: individuals, rather than systems of law, gender, class or race, become responsible for the crimes under consideration (Benedict 1992).

Including experts' views increases the legitimacy of news stories about rape, but it also has a serious effect on the discussion of rape law reform initiatives. Since trials are the focal point of coverage, trial attorneys—who may have a range of experiences with, understandings of, and positions on rape law reform—are most often sought for comment. In the three cases under discussion, trial attorneys were repeatedly featured as experts whose comments could add legitimacy to news stories. In two cases, this tended to further disadvantage the articulation of reform ideas, since attorneys were unconcerned with, unaware of, or even hostile toward, law reform initiatives. In addition, attorneys are most often asked to comment on the trial at hand rather than on its relation to a larger project or cultural context. When the trials chosen for coverage have no particularly significant relation to law reform initiatives (as explained previously), reporters are even less likely to ask attorneys about larger reform issues and do not seek out commentary by law reformers.

Thus, the selection of trials for their popular or dramatic content, in combination with the conventions of news coverage, operates to contain the dispersal of new meanings about rape, its victims, and its perpetrators. By the time rape laws change and public trials receive national attention, feminist law reformers are by definition not the central experts, and therefore their perspective is seldom explained in any coherent way. As a consequence, the social movement strategy of mainstreaming oppositional ideas by seeking legal changes limits the speed with which the movement's arguments are presented in mainstream news: alternative constructions or ideas, in this case regarding rape, can only slowly work their way into a widespread and sympathetic national discussion. The inclusion of rape law reformers, such as crisis center workers, who have recently been consulted more often as peripheral experts, is a sign that reform ideas are gaining legitimacy.

Legitimation of Rape Reform Ideas in Mainstream News

With all of the factors impeding the expression of the ideas of social change movements in mainstream news, how is it possible for such ideas to *enter* the national dialogue? If mainstream news functions to negotiate social change issues for the dominant ideology, then some oppositional ideas must be incorporated or accepted into this discourse. If news serves to signal an acceptance or rejection of various elements of social change ideologies into the mainstream, what elements of rape reform ideology are being accepted, and how is this accomplished? What elements of reform remain outside mainstream news constructions of rape? There are several points of entry in news coverage of issue-oriented trials.

Media focus on trial testimony reflects trial strategy and as such incorporates reformed rape laws. If an attorney understands rape law reform and finds it useful in the case at hand, then her or his argument to the court may contain some elements of reform that are subsequently reported in the news. Although evidence is most often presented without commentary or a legal or social framework, news coverage does include evidence by both sides at trial, and as long as the testimony of both defense and prosecution witnesses is included in coverage, this testimony will *reflect* changing laws and the strategies of both sides in the case. Even though news reports will seldom discuss trial strategy in relation to reform goals and ideas, the testimony based implicitly on those new notions will be reported. Journalists are generally conscientious about reporting evidence on each side of the case, and as the rules of evidence change, so does the content of news coverage. News also tends to include basic elements of trial strategy, such as "force" versus "consent," which may change as a result of rape reform efforts.

As the reform movement gains credibility, its experts will increasingly be asked for comment in news coverage. Reform beliefs can also be aired if the prosecuting attorney articulates them, if reformers are consulted as peripheral experts, or if special stories on reform are written in the context of heightened national interest in rape resulting from the publicity of a particular trial. Occasionally, a director of a rape crisis line or other "expert" not involved specifically with the case will be quoted. Also, reporters seeking new angles may write stories about rape law reform itself, using the current trial merely as a starting point for a retrospective examination. Though few in number, these stories solicit the majority of feminist commentary.

The rape trial offers some built-in advantages and opportunities for the expression of the disparate views on rape, and news coverage of the three cases in this study has clearly demonstrated the active process through which each view has gained discursive priority at various times and in various ways. This chapter explicates the struggle for acceptance and the specific ways in which legitimacy has been achieved for both the traditional and reformed views in coverage of each of these three cases.

In all three cases news coverage was dramatic and personalized, focusing on the individual trial participants. News also quoted trial attorneys as the relevant expert sources, usually without thorough or meaningful explanations of context or systems of reasoning or understanding. Yet each case created a space for expressing new ideas about rape based on the victim's perspective. Although the reform view almost never received a coherent depiction in mainstream news, in two of the three cases this coverage clearly accepted some *element* of rape reform ideology as one of the many truths about rape.

All three cases received extensive national coverage in straight news reports, editorials, and syndicated commentaries throughout the duration of the legal proceedings. The analysis that follows focuses primarily on straight news stories and nationally syndicated columns, which together represent the news discourse most widely available and include accounts of the people, events, ideas, and dramatic turns that formed the public's understanding of the trials' significant elements. Sources include large circulation newspapers such as the *Washington Post, Chicago Tribune,* and *New York Times*; local newspapers such as the *Salem Capital Journal, San Francisco Chronicle,* and *Oregon Statesman*; national newsmagazines such as *Time, Newsweek,* and *People*; and the national news broadcasts of CBS, NBC, and ABC.

News Coverage of *Rideout*

As the first issue-oriented rape case to receive national media attention, the Rideout case clearly illustrates the limits to incorporating reform ideas into mainstream public discussion. The question of character framed most news coverage: the case unfolded as a traditional story of a manipulative woman seeking either revenge or fame in bringing her charge of rape, and the defendant was portrayed as a confused husband seemingly incapable of the malicious act with which he was charged. Nonetheless, commentators seemed to agree that marital rape was wrong, and support for the goals behind the new law were frequently expressed.

News stories portrayed John Rideout as young and vulnerable: a "thin dark-haired man, the traces of acne still on his cheeks, staring up at [Greta] with wide brown eyes that rarely blinked" (Gorney 1979, 2). He was a simple, working-class "loser" who had trouble understanding his own problems. Greta Rideout, on the other hand, was depicted as a stronger and more intelligent individual with a complicated sexual past and a desire for fame and fortune: "an occasionally unscrupulous young woman capable of lying, teasing, and plotting to get what she wanted" (Gorney 1979, 2). She was depicted as the classic manipulative, lying "victim." Relations of power based on gender and economics faded away as news characterizations contrasted Greta's strength and savvy with John's ineptitude and romantic awkwardness.

Coverage of the Rideout case, especially local coverage, stuck closely to trial testimony about Greta's character. Excerpts of quotes by the numerous witnesses were included in the coverage on each day of the trial, with only fragmentary references to the efforts and goals of rape law reform. Greta Rideout's sexual history, her motivations for bringing the charge, and a description of her general character were brought into question in news headlines even before the start of the trial. As many observers noted, she was on trial as much as her husband, and her history and behavior became much more relevant than his. District Attorney Gary Gortmaker commented publicly that "in any rape trial the alleged victim is likely to have untold psychological pressures placed upon her," adding that in this case "we're going to try the victim first, the law second, and the defendant third" ("Different Focus," 1978b, 7A).

Although important legal issues in marital rape law were being argued in the Rideout case, media coverage rarely explained how equal protection of wives would necessitate the elimination of the marital rape exemption. Seldom was legal reasoning connected with evidence or claims of guilt and innocence. When news accounts did outline the legal crux of the case, it was usually with brief reference to "force" versus "consent," contrasting Greta's account of violence with John's account of mutual consent. The lack of a clear analysis of the legal issues, and an overemphasis on dramatic elements such as the exaggerated relevance of character evidence, reinforced the traditional focus on the victim's credibility and personal life that rape law reformers had tried to eliminate in trial practice. Although the trial included ample testimony of this kind, and thereby reinforced the bias, news coverage was equally responsible for underscoring this tenacious legal prejudice. Without connection to legal reasoning, the implication in *Rideout* coverage was that character evidence was sufficient to prove John Rideout's innocence.

The presentation of the prosecution and defense attorneys' "expert" commentary virtually eliminated the articulation of rape law reform from news coverage of the trial. Defense attorney Charles Burt was quoted far more frequently than District Attorney Gary Gortmaker, and quotes from Gortmaker did not illuminate the goals and implications of rape law reform. News reports of the Rideout case constrained the circulation of reform meanings of rape more thoroughly than coverage of either of the other two cases, perhaps because the case seemingly fit the traditional construction of an unjustified claim of rape. The case was reported in the media on the basis of the mythic criteria that had previously been established for rape cases. Nonetheless, mainstream coverage provided a forum where support for the substance of the legal change in question could be expressed, and as such, it articulated a shift in mainstream understandings of marital rape. News discourse largely accepted the concept of marital rape but left the appropriateness of the legal solution in doubt.

Coming to Terms with Marital Rape

In the news coverage, the case evoked a tension between commitments to fairness on one hand and to tradition and precedent on the other: discussions of the case and of marital rape revealed a consensus that the marital contract did not imply consent to sex whenever and however a husband might desire it. Many observers commented to the effect that "an end to the common-law notion that rape is permissible in marriage is long overdue" ("Marriage, Rape and the Law," 1978, 22.1). Columnist George Will asserted that "the idea that marriage implies or requires perpetual consent, under all circumstances, to sex is grotesque" (Will 1978). William Raspberry agreed that the concept made sense: "I suppose that nearly everybody believes it is theoretically possible for a man to rape his wife: to make her believe that he will do her serious bodily harm unless she acquiesces to his sexual demands" (Raspberry 1979, 32). And one San Francisco newspaper headline announced, "Readers Favor a Rape Law" (1978, 1). A general acceptance that marital rape could occur implied a need for new standards for judging and evaluating rape, rapists, and victims, but news coverage did not discuss such criteria.

The first nationally covered trial to involve marital rape, the *Rideout* case was typical of many marital rape situations in that the Rideouts' marriage was marked by a history of violence. While information about wife battering syndrome and the prevalence and seriousness of marital rape was available from non-mainstream sources (for example, in Del Martin's *Battered Wives* [1976]), feminist reformers were not routinely sought for their insights, since their views were not yet widely accepted as a way of understanding violence in marriage.[1]

The same journalists who expressed acceptance of the concept "marital rape" were unable to imagine how the new law could effectively be enforced, rendering it theoretically correct but practically ineffective. If the concept of the husband rapist was accepted, the rapist could no longer be viewed only as a brutal, deranged, or marginalized stranger. Rape could no longer be characterized as a random crime of sexual frustration and anger, and victims could no longer be perceived as young virgins innocently caught up in the sick fantasies of rampaging criminals. The need for revised understandings of rapists and victims was sometimes granted explicit recognition, and writers struggled visibly with issues of definition and character. One writer noted that "in the marital context, predicated as it is on sexual interchange and complex emotional bonds, the lines of guilt and responsibility become blurred" ("Rape in Marriage," 1978, 1). Others agreed that marital rape might be a serious problem but also concluded that it would be a complex area for the legal system to decide. George Will worried that when the law entered private relationships there was "quicksand all around"; he warned that "it is a grave business when the law empowers one partner to charge another with a felony punishable by 20 years in prison" (Will 1978), echoing Hale's warnings that rape was a special crime and that revenge was a likely motive for false claims.

Generally, warnings like Will's about the possibility of false claims were only vague suggestions. The *New York Times* noted that "juries will always have to weigh the word of the husband against the wife with virtually no corroborating evidence" and that "such problems are likely to deter many such prosecutions" ("Marriage, Rape and the Law," 1978, 22.1). Women deserved protection, but when and how to provide it had not been resolved. A local Oregon newspaper report at the end of the trial noted that John Rideout had been acquitted "as he had to be, because no jury could know, beyond a reasonable doubt, what transpired in the emotion-fraught minutes around which the case was centered" ("Rideout Case Shows Limitations of System," 1978, 6D). In short, in order to accept a wholesale feminist view of marital violence, mainstream commentators needed to overcome traditional beliefs about rape: they would have had to believe that wife battering syndrome existed, that there was no significant motivation for a wife to concoct a false story of rape, that juries were no less able to decide who was telling the truth in a rape case than in any other case, and that rapists were not only violent strangers but also "loving" husbands.

The dominant framework for understanding rape, based on male experiences and fears of false accusation, was still evident. As William Raspberry noted, "nearly every man knows (or thinks he knows) of women who say no, no, no when what they mean is: Force me. A few men still believe that every woman wants to be raped, that 'gentle' and 'considerate' are equally namby-pamby" (Raspberry 1979, 32). By this logic, a husband-rapist would have to be extremely violent and unrepentant, going well beyond acting out this traditional notion of heterosexual sex and demonstrating that he was well outside the realm of any "normal" male perspective on the subject. The portrayal of John Rideout as a man with a sincere but confused character suggested that while he might be old-fashioned or clumsy he was not vicious or dangerous. The traditional understanding of rape was still current and familiar enough to portray the John Rideout verdict as an unambiguous one.

Resistance to Rape Reform Arguments in Mainstream News

The most thorough discussions of trial strategy and the issues surrounding rape law reform initiatives occurred before or at the start of the trial (see Furey 1978a, 1978a; Liddick 1978). After the trial began, however, media coverage linked character testimony to motive only loosely if at all, even in those stories that focused narrowly on Greta's character. While numerous articles mentioned that a new bill had been passed, few included the legal reasoning that justified it. Typical comments were confined to the observation that John was the first man in the country to be tried for raping his wife while living with her (Evenson 1978h), or that the central issue was whether intercourse was forcible or consensual ("Rideouts' Home Life Described," 1978). After the start of the trial, even a story entitled "The Background" stated only that the bill was originally introduced with a spousal exemption and changed to allow prosecution of husbands as well. Rather than including the rationale behind the new bill, this article quoted Oregon Senator Vern Cook, who had voted against it. Cook explained that he opposed the bill because "a woman has a responsibility to avoid a situation in the first place by moving out of the house" and that he feared that trials would amount to "a swearing contest between husband and wife" that would be difficult to adjudicate (Rede 1978a, 1C). A few network stories did a better job of including brief descriptions of the goals of rape reform as well as the objections to the new law (Kennedy, 19 December 1978; Petersen, 18 December 1978).

Throughout the trial Greta's character was attacked in headline after headline: "Witnesses Say Greta Expected Riches and Fame" (Furey 1978d), "Two Rape Witnesses Declare Accuser Lied" (1978), "Defense Attorney's Questioning Challenges Mrs. Rideout's Honesty" (Evenson 1978b), "Defense Argues That Mrs. Rideout Seeking 'Fame, Fortune' from Case" (Evenson 1978a), "Wife's Credibility at Issue in Rape" (1978), and "Rideout Still Uncertain of Wife's Relationships" (Evenson 1978f). The articles emphasized the most dramatic aspects of testimony regarding Greta's sexual past. Witnesses were quoted as testifying that Greta had said she was going to be "rich and famous" (Evenson 1978a) and that she had baited John with a lesbian fantasy that was untrue (Furey, "Mrs. Rideout Lied to Her Husband" 1978b). A brief *New York Times* story noted that "Charles Burt told jurors in his opening statement that Mrs. Rideout had told her husband that she had had a lesbian relationship with her friend" and that Jack Hinckle, John's step-brother, had "denied" Greta's previous accusation that he had raped her ("Two Rape Trial Witnesses," 1978). In addition, news stories featured testimony that she had had two abortions, and that she had threatened her husband with the new law. A 22 December 1978 *Salem Capital Journal* article described the testimony of two key witnesses at length (Furey 1978b). One testified that Greta had fabricated a story about a lesbian fantasy to "bait" John. Another claimed that Greta had falsely accused him of rape and later retracted the accusation. Even after the prosecution's opening statement and testimony from two police officers on the first day of the trial, an *Oregon Statesman* story quoted portions of the closed *pretrial* hearing only, to feature more dramatic and scurrilous details about Greta's sexual fantasies and history and include Burt's comment that "this young lady has a serious sexual problem . . . she will try to justify her activities by any means she can" (Evenson 1978a, 6C).

Nearly every account of the trial included character testimony about Greta; a majority of articles foregrounded this testimony by including it in the first few paragraphs of the story and by devoting disproportionate space to it. The information that Greta had previously accused Hinckle of rape and then retracted her story, that she had told John of a lesbian fantasy as if it were real, and that she had had two abortions continued to be reported in numerous stories after their original appearance on the day the testimony was heard. Near the end of the trial, NBC summarized character evidence against Greta that included the lesbian fantasy story and her previous claim of rape (Sternoff, 27 December 1978).

In effect, Greta's characterization in the media did not fit the "appropriate" profile of the innocent rape victim. The large number of witnesses giving sensationalistic testimony about Greta's character provided abundant material for media coverage. Although information about Greta's sexual history and about her alleged threat to John was legally relevant only in relation to motive (and only to the extent that it showed Greta had filed rape charges for profit or revenge), news stories seldom discussed this connection. The "objective" inclusion of direct testimony in press reports offered up sexual history evidence as an end in itself, with no legal framework for understanding its significance.

News writers, speaking for and to the American public, did not examine the necessary redefinitions of marriage, "rapist," and "victim" that might eventually render marital rape a useful and logical concept. A fully articulated reform understanding of marital rape would necessarily have been at odds with the elements of the traditional formulation of rape used to structure news stories and glean meaningful facts from the trial. For the most part, mainstream news coverage of this trial did not acknowledge Greta's account of the rape and the violence that had preceded it, although some stories did quote Greta on the subject of marital violence. More typically, her motives for bringing the charge were mentioned primarily in the context of how they were "in question." *The New York Times*, linking motive to evidence in an unusually clear way after the trial's start, noted only that numerous witnesses had raised doubts about Greta's motives in accusing her husband and that "there has been discussion as to whether she has been seeking monetary reward or vengeance" (Ledbetter 1978b, A14). An explicit discussion of how pursuing a rape charge would exact vengeance or of how a monetary reward would be a factor was not included. For the character evidence to make sense, readers had to be able to fill in their own connections between it and the innocence or guilt of the Rideouts. This could be done easily by anyone familiar with traditional ideas about rape.

A *CBS Morning News* report typified the coverage by making only loose connections between the argument and the evidence introduced. On the first day of the trial, Barry Petersen's story reported the following:

Petersen: Defense Attorney Charles Burt characterized Mrs. Rideout as a woman with serious sexual problems, saying, "The entire incident is a great gratification to Greta. She has been in the limelight." He said a movie company offered her $60,000 for her story. Rideout sat quietly as his attorney said there was sexual intercourse that night, but not forcible rape. Burt talked of testimony that will show how Mrs. Rideout had also accused her husband's stepbrother of rape, a charge the stepbrother denies. The jury listened intently as he said Greta claimed she had a lesbian relationship, then claimed she only made that up to taunt her husband. Burt was asked why the testimony was necessary. *Charles Burt*: Well, I think it's important because my client contends that he did not forcibly have relations with her; important to know how much veracity she has. *Gary Gortmaker*: Well, state's theory is that the marriage contract is not a shield to responsibility, because it is no different to the victim whether you're raped after a marriage contract or before. (Petersen, 21 December 1978)

In this and other reports during the proceedings, no mention was made of Greta's motive *per se*. Instead, Burt called Greta's "veracity" into question as a justification for the introduction of sexual history evidence. At the same time, the district attorney offered no counterbalancing story to the defense's account (at least none was included in the story), suggesting only that the marriage contract was not a license to rape. Other accounts quoted Gortmaker's assertion that women had a right to be safe from harm within marriage (Kennedy, 19 December 1978). Although Gortmaker's comments emphasized equal protection, the reform notion that sexual history evidence and interpersonal behavior of the victim do not nullify a rape claim was not articulated in these reports. Questions of credibility and motivation remained.

On the second day of the trial, Petersen reported:

> The prosecution called a dozen witnesses, some of them people the defense had found and planned to use later in the trial. One such witness was Doug Lowe, an upstairs neighbor. . . . Lowe told the jury about an argument in his presence between John and Greta the night before the alleged incident. According to Lowe, Greta mentioned the new law to John, who said he knew nothing about it. Then, Lowe testified, Greta said, "Well, John, one of these days you're going to go too far and you're going to find out about it. . . ." Defense attorney Charles Burt said later he thinks Lowe's testimony was more beneficial to the defense than to the prosecution. *Charles Burt*: We understand that the jury is going to have to decide who to believe, and we think the fact that she may have a motive for bringing this charge, other than the truth, is important. (Petersen, 22 December 1978)

The idea that Greta's motive was in question was acknowledged, but with no information as to what this other motive might be. Revenge was the implied motive, but no coverage spelled out why Greta would be seeking revenge against John (if it was for beating her repeatedly, then this would seem relevant to the case).

The central question of forcible compulsion versus consent was noted in numerous stories. During the trial, evidence suggesting there had been a rape was presented in a fragmented way, as it occurred in the trial testimony, and it was summarized only rarely within a single news story. Stories that described specific testimony regarding physical injuries and other evidence suggestive of rape did not link it to the overall concept of "forcible compulsion." A typical article citing witnesses supportive of Greta's version quoted one as saying that "I could hear muffled sounds, as if someone was trying to scream, but couldn't" and that "her lips looked liked they'd been bleeding . . . her eye was red and the side of her face was swollen" (Evenson 1978b, 8A); yet the piece never explained how this might be related to forcible compulsion or consent (see Evenson 1978g). John admitted tampering with Greta's car so she could not escape, "slapping" her and causing bruises on her face, and then engaging in intercourse with her. A neighbor testified that she heard a car engine roaring and later "saw John Rideout go to the car. . . . He got out of the car, opened the hood and took out something. . . . He tried to start it up, but it wouldn't start" (Evenson 1978d, 1A). Testimony of the rape crisis counselor and the physician who examined Greta also suggested that there had been forcible compulsion. Greta called the police immediately following the incident, telling them, "I don't want to go down to my apartment . . . my husband just got through beating me. . . . I ran away from him. And I was running through the garden and he got ahold of me" ("Greta Rideout's Police Call Brought to Jury's Attention," 1978). In addition, reports that quoted Greta's testimony carried evidence of forcible compulsion. Greta asserted that John "beat her into submission" (Ledbetter 1978b, A14) and that she thought her jaw would break if she were hit again (Evenson 1978g, 6C).

Evidence that a rape had occurred was reported, but much less frequently and prominently than evidence to the contrary. While several local stories focused exclusively on testimony against Greta's character (Furey 1978b; Evenson 1978c, 1978f, 1978h; "Two Rape Trial Witnesses Declare Accuser Lied," 1978), stories focusing exclusively on evidence in support of her charge were much rarer. However, several stories after the close of the trial did give balanced summaries of the evidence regarding the force versus consent issue (Footlick 1979; Petersen, 27 December 1978).

While Greta was portrayed in terms that identified an illegitimate claimant, news coverage during and after the trial emphasized John's gentleness and lack of intelligence. The coverage also focused on the Rideouts as a couple with a shared experience of the trial events. John was mentioned far less frequently than Greta, and references to him were generally unflattering but suggestive of passivity rather than malice. The most frequent characterization of John was drawn from the testimony of his sister-in-law, who stated that he was "inquisitive, bright, not a strong personality, friendly, out-going" and also "gentle" and "very passive" (Evenson 1978e, 8A). Some reports also mentioned John's mother, and one quoted her comment about John's new job at a "Salem Pancake Restaurant": "He's already doing better than most twenty-one-year olds" (Mitchell 1978, A8). His brother, a penitentiary employee, testified that John needed help but would not get what he needed in jail (Furey 1978c). When John's appearance and demeanor were described, he most often came off as someone not sophisticated enough to plan or carry out a violent crime. References were also made to his "opportunities 'to move up' at Sambo's" restaurant (Rosenberg 1978, 1A), and to his simple outlook on the trial.

John was further portrayed as somewhat simple, young and naive, traditional, and caring. A *CBS News* description of him during the trial noted: "Rideout sat, his head occasionally bowed, as Lowe remembered a moment in the argument when Greta left the room. John said, 'I love her very much. What am I doing wrong? Something is not going right. I love her. I love her'" (Petersen, 22 December 1978). Consistent portrayals of John as sincere but confused rendered him an unlikely rapist.

He simply did not appear to have the wherewithal to orchestrate either a violent rape or an elaborate lie.

John's innocence was indirectly suggested by continued references to the Rideouts as people who shared the same problems. Throughout the trial proceedings, the Rideouts were often referred to as a naive couple torn apart by events beyond their control. On the final day of the trial, the *Salem Capital Journal* reported that "a prevailing sentiment among many watching the Rideout trial was that of sympathy for both people involved," and characterized them as "a young married couple, burdened with emotional, sexual, and financial problems throughout their stormy two years of marriage" (Furey, 1978c, 1A). This report also underscored John's innocence: he too was a victim, just as much as Greta. Headlines such as "'Ordinary Couple' Split by Marital Rape Trial in Oregon" (Mitchell 1978) and "Rideouts Have Both Suffered" (Furey 1978c) emphasized the shared experiences of the husband and wife, suggesting further that, in this case anyway, a husband could not really be the same as a rapist. According to traditional definitions, John Rideout was not a rapist and Greta was not an appropriate victim.

Frequent citing of the trial's lead attorneys on both sides worked to suppress rape reform ideas because neither attorney clearly addressed them. After demonstrating that Greta had a "serious sexual problem," the defense strategy minimized the seriousness of the Rideout marital struggles and asserted that these "fight, kiss and make up" episodes did not belong in court. Emphasizing the "marriage gone wrong" interpretation, Burt asserted that "this is not a classic case of men's rights versus women's rights" (Ledbetter 1978a, A1). Picking up on this theme, one headline posed the central question as "A Rape—Or Marital Tiff?" Another article that promised a view of the "married life of the Rideouts" began by reiterating that "Greta Mary Rideout, who charged her husband with rape, has 'a very serious sexual problem' that neither she nor her husband 'could understand or solve,' a defense attorney contended Wednesday" (Evenson 1978c). The primary news angle in these stories centered on the Rideouts' troubled relationship rather than on the possible criminal nature of John's actions.

By arguing that this case was open to widely varying interpretations (see "A Rape—Or Marital Tiff?" in the *Oakland Tribune*), the defense was able to emphasize the futility of trying "these cases" in court. For defense attorney Burt—as for many commentators on the case—marital rape might be characterized in a number of ways: as a marital tiff, as the result of youthful whim, as evidence of changing emotions in a rocky marital relationship, as the charge of an angry and vengeful wife, or as any combination thereof. Observers expressed concern that the new law would "burden the taxpayer and the courts by allowing any woman to yell rape just because she's mad at her old man" or that "domestic fights that go into rape charges would really clog the court calendars" ("Readers Favor a Rape Law," 1979, 1). Burt was quoted as fearing that a conviction in this case would result in a "flock" of similar cases, and that the Rideouts often had physical fights but "frequently made up after a quarrel by making love" (quoted in Mitchell 1978, A8). He also elicited testimony from Jack Hinckle to the effect that the Rideouts "played games" by chasing each other around the house before lovemaking. Reports of this evidence, seldom accompanied by descriptions of the actual incident, further suggested that the marital relationship could not easily be adjudicated through rape law. Burt's comments fit into the traditional framework of understanding.

Without a coherent alternative for understanding Greta's actions and motives in bringing her charge against John, character evidence underscored the validity of the traditional interpretation that posited confusion, manipulation, and personal gain as motives. Three months after the trial, a *Time* magazine article discussed rape law reform, summarized the Michigan statute, and contrasted traditional and reformed ideas. This report included no quotes and concluded that the Rideout case illustrated "the difficulty" posed by marital rape law because the Rideouts were reconciled after the trial ("Revolution in Rape," 1979c, 50). As Helen Benedict (1992) observes, reporters did not follow up on the story beyond the frequently noted reconciliation. Indeed, on the whole, the news media had concluded that the Rideout case proved the truth of everyone's worst fears about marital rape cases.

Rape Law Reform: An Opening in Mainstream News Coverage of the Rideout Case

In spite of all the limitations on coverage of rape law reform in news reports of the Rideout trial, there were, nonetheless, some openings for the expression of a new perspective on rape. The admission that rape could potentially occur within marriage and that wives deserved protection from it was not insignificant: centuries of common law and "common sense" dictated that married women gave up a variety of rights enjoyed by single women and all men. Likewise, beliefs about heterosexual sexuality, such as that echoed by William Raspberry (every man thinks he knows a woman who says no but means "force me" [1979]), made many commentators hesitant to accept what they saw as the possibility that a husband could be found guilty and punished for a simple misunderstanding.

The reform view found some points of entry beyond the acknowledgment that rape in marriage could happen, however, both in the use, however infrequent, of feminists as sources of expert commentary and in fleeting acknowledgments that Greta Rideout was not alone in her experience of violence within marriage.

Feminists were quoted firsthand in some stories, although with one exception (Liddick 1978) their comments were extremely limited. One woman gave an indirect description of equal protection: she was quoted as saying that the law presented a problem for women before 1977, since only women legally separated from their husbands could bring a charge of rape (" 'Rape Law' Changed by Oregon Solons," 1978). Another story quoted a coordinator of Oregon crisis lines as saying, "We [women] have been taught that we have no choice, that [sexual submission] is our role in life, what we're supposed to do. . . . This trial is so important to make women aware they're not property, that they have choices" (Mitchell 1978, A8), thereby implying that evolving social roles were a good reason to change the marital exemption to rape. Several broadcast news reports carried the comment that the marital rape concept was a strong one and that feminists were "not going to back off" from it; however, these reports gave no explanation as to why the concept was so strong or what it entailed. An Oregon crisis center worker commented after the end of the trial that she was "terrifically saddened by the verdict and concerned about the future of women who have to live with marital violence every day" ("Rape? No," 1979a, 61).

Other intimations were made that marital violence did exist and that Greta was not alone in her experience of it. After the trial, Greta was quoted as saying, "Now men a lot worse than John are just sitting back and snickering," and "a lot of women who are beaten a lot worse than I was beaten and forced into sex afterwards were waiting to see whether a man could be convicted and punished for what men are doing to them" ("Wife Has No Regrets," 1978). Several network stories carried her comments on marital rape. ABC quoted her version of events leading up to the incident in question: "I felt like I was in Hell. I was suffering. I was married to him for two years and the violence got worse month by month" (Kennedy, 19 December 1978; see also Sternoff, 19 December 1978). Her statements highlighted the differences between male and female perspectives on the issues of marital violence and rape. In addition, Gary Gortmaker observed that he had seen other "Rideout cases," but that they "usually end up in one of two ways: suicide or homicide" (Sternoff, 22 December 1978). Nancy Burch of the Salem Women's Crisis Center was briefly quoted on the "astounding proportions" of marital violence (Bonventre 1979, 55) and on the "archaic notion that a woman is her husband's property" ("Against a Wife's Will," 1 January 1979). These suggestions of widespread marital violence and rape were not enough to clearly define marital rape or to specify how the law could cope with it, but they did bring a formerly personal issue into the public arena, thereby helping to validate it for discussion.

In the Rideout case, an airing of reform views was limited by an emphasis on character evidence that fit into the traditional framework for understanding rape, a reluctance to discuss either legal or reform reasoning on marital violence, and a narrow focus on attorneys' comments about the trial's implications and significance. Frequently voiced fears about the special nature of marital rape with relation to the jury system and the law were not usually counterbalanced with explanations used by those who had urged the passage of the new law or voted for it. Overall, male fears about false accusations and unjust punishment for minor misunderstandings prevailed in the construction of the case in mainstream news. Feminist ideas, on the other hand, found limited expression in references to marital violence and in the use of rape law reformers as (infrequent) sources of expert commentary.

In the absence of an alternative understanding of marital rape, and in the face of traditional myths about the "special nature" of rape, with its emphasis on corroboration and the truthfulness of the key witness, it is not surprising that mainstream writers and commentators had difficulty with this case. If "consent" could not be determined in nonmarital cases, it would be even more difficult to establish in the Rideout trial. If vengeance was a motive for victims to fabricate claims of rape, then intimate knowledge of the accused could only make this motive more salient. If rape charges were sometimes the result of misunderstandings or differences of interpretation, then marital rape cases only multiplied the possibilities of frivolous and unfair claims of rape against innocent men. Finally, if rapes were mostly thought to be the result of violent attacks on unsuspecting women by lurking strangers, then a husband was by definition not a rapist. The logic of the new law was acceptable: in theory a husband did not deserve the right to abuse his wife with impunity. Yet the terms in which this new law could be rendered useful or protective to wives were not to be found in mainstream news coverage of this case.

News Coverage of the Big Dan's Case

Four years after the close of the Rideout case, the Big Dan's rape trial made national headlines for several weeks. As in coverage of the Rideout case, national news coverage of the Big Dan's case expressed support for an important element of the reformed view of rape. However, as with Rideout, this legitimation took place at the expense of a more expansive or coherent understanding of the goals and ideas of rape law reform.

The conduct and outcome of the trial, and some elements of the media coverage, were radically different from that of the Rideout case. Since this case involved six defendants, news coverage could not focus primarily on the defendants' character. With regard to the Big Dan's defendants, there was a continued focus on dramatic and personal information, but coverage also shifted slightly toward their Portuguese heritage and community. In addition, sexual history evidence was excluded from the trial, thus eliminating the source of much "character" evidence about the victim and significantly altering the coverage of that element of the case. Some stories indicated confusion about why sexual history evidence was disallowed. Although many stories questioned the victim's character, many others included only positive or neutral information about her background and behavior.

Whereas the Rideouts' relationship provided much of the drama in the news coverage, the focus in this case was on the dramatic elements of the rape and of the angry protests of both Portuguese and feminist groups. The Big Dan's trial also involved important legal matters not necessarily related to rape: the issues of cameras in the courtroom and alleged media and judicial bias against the Portuguese defendants became the focus of much of the coverage. Although rape law reform was one of many issues relevant to the case, the majority of stories on the trial did not mention law reform efforts at all.

But possibly the most significant difference between the Big Dan's case and the Rideout case was that there was an eye-witness to the Big Dan's rape. In one sense, overwhelming corroborating evidence made this an easy case: no matter what the victim's past or character, the bar owner testified that she was screaming and crying while some of the men raped her. As in Rideout, a media "verdict" was implied throughout coverage of the case, but this time the decision was in favor of the prosecution rather than the defense. There were indications during the Big Dan's trial that the victim had lied, cheated on welfare, and brought a previous complaint of rape, yet these facts seldom made the headlines as they had in *Rideout.* In most national media stories, the victim in this case was referred to as a "21-year-old mother of two."

There is no question that the victim in this case suffered greatly, as Helen Benedict (1992) documents at length: she was harassed, threatened, and eventually hounded out of town after CNN revealed her name and several newspapers followed suit. In this light, it is especially noteworthy that news coverage focused on her perseverance and strength, and on the important role of a victim's testimony in gaining justice in rape cases. If anything, this case was an eloquent argument for victims *not* to tell their stories. While this was recognized in a number of broadcast stories, news coverage and commentaries generally emphasized the idea that coming forward and testifying at trial were the right things to do.

Early descriptions of the crime provided some drama by often exaggerating sensational elements:

Twenty-five hundred people turned out to protest the gang rape of a 21-year-old woman in a bar in the fishing town of New Bedford. Witnesses say four men raped the woman on a pool table for at least two hours while a dozen or more other men watched, did nothing to intervene, or whistled and cheered. No one phoned the police. The woman received no help until she finally struggled free, and half naked, made it to the street. (Currier, 15 May 1983)

Pretrial reports such as this one emphasized details to add to the dramatic effect of the story. As the trial progressed, reports reduced the total number of cheering men to fewer than ten. Some of the initial news reports had been based on the police report, which in turn had been based on the statement of the hysterical victim on the night of the rape.

Coverage of the crime, when it centered on the victim's testimony, became even more dramatic: "A 22-year-old woman told a jury today that she had been pinned down and raped on a pool table in Big Dan's Tavern while several people ignored her screams. 'I was screaming—I was begging for help,' the woman said. . . . 'I could hear people laughing and cheering, yelling,' she said" ("Court in New Bedford Hears Woman's Testimony," 1984, 12A). Even some later coverage dramatized the crime in its descriptions: "Four men committed 'an explosion of violence and brutality against that small woman,' a prosecutor said today in urging a jury to convict the men of raping a woman on a barroom pool table" ("Reports to Police Questioned," 1984, A18).

Coverage of this case was less personalized than in *Rideout,* in part because the victim's identity was concealed in most reports. Descriptions of her character, while present in virtually all stories of the trial, were much less harsh than those of Greta Rideout. Less attention was given to testimony about the victim's character, and thus it was given less credibility, as the following excerpts show:

Well, the—alleged victim has been on the stand most of the week, and the defense attorneys have been picking away at her credibility, basically trying to paint her as less than a pillar of the community. And I would say they've been rather effective in doing that. And the tavern barkeeper was also on the stand yesterday, and he seemed to add some credence to some of the testimony that she had had earlier in the week [sic]. So that's where we are at this point. (Currier, 2 March 1984)

The woman . . . denied under cross-examination . . . that she had told another woman in Big Dan's that she was seeing a psychiatrist. ("Reports to Police Questioned," 1984, A18)

The defense for one of six men charged with the barroom rape of a young mother rested today after a medical expert testified that the woman was "clinically poisoned with alcohol" the night of the incident. ("Defense Ends for One of Six," 1984)

Using a mixture of loud voices, dramatic gestures and penetrating stares, the defense team has repeatedly tried to chip away at the victim's credibility, trying to portray her as a liar, a welfare cheat, a person with mental problems and as a promiscuous woman who is out to make money on a lawsuit she has filed against the bar owners and the bartender, Mr. Machado. . . .
The attempts to damage her credibility confirm fears expressed by her lawyer and by women's groups. (Rangel 1984a, 1.6)

Defense attorneys argued that the "victim"—whose identity is being protected by the court—had flirted with the men in Big Dan's tavern and encouraged their sexual advances. They suggested that she had embellished the rape story to win a lawsuit and a lucrative book contract, and accused her of welfare fraud. Finally, they contended that this was not the first time. . . .
The woman admitted she had illegally received welfare checks for three years. But she denied the other charges and clung to her story: two men had raped her and a third had tried to perform oral sex while the bar patrons cheered "like it was a baseball game." (Starr 1984, 21)

Although some evidence of this type was included in many stories, damaging character evidence was usually limited to one or two sentences in stories that did not focus on her cross-examination testimony. Damaging testimony was also often summarized rather than directly quoted, and defense strategy was highlighted as much as the results of that strategy. When the victim was mentioned in passing, she was usually referred to as a young mother of two or as a twenty-one- (or twenty-two-) year-old mother of two. More than fifteen *New York Times* stories used such phrases to refer to the victim. One such story asserted that the town of New Bedford was "stunned and embittered last March when six men were charged with raping the mother of two children on a pool table in Big Dan's bar" (Rangel 1984c, 22). An article in *People* magazine reported that she had refused sleeping medication since the incident because she wanted to be alert if her children cried. The article went on to note that the victim got her mind off the trauma of the rape by caring for her children (Vespa 1984, 81).

These stories were sympathetic to the victim, and some implied that she did not desire or deserve what had happened to her. *Newsweek* ran an article entitled "New Bedford Rape: Rejecting the Myth." "The myth" was the idea that women always ask for rape, and the article concluded with a quote from Prosecutor Raymond Veary who pleaded, "take away her innocence if you must. But don't take away her humanity" (Goldman et al. 1984, 39). In another report, the victim's attorney explained the difficulty posed by the use of sexual history testimony as evidence of "character": "this is a perfect case study of what women have to go through in rape trials . . . her entire past is laid open" (Rangel 1984b, A10). District Attorney Kane asserted on *CBS News,* "I think it's gonna operate as a deterrent against women coming forward, and I—and I—and I fear for rape victims in the future" (Kurtis, 23 March 1984). Asserting that "however imprudent it may have been for her to have been in Big Dan's under those circumstances," the *National Review* concluded that "she had every legal right to be there" ("Big Dan's Tavern," 1984, 20). One story even suggested that the victim was a heroine for her bravery and courage during the ordeal since she had felt anger rather than shame or guilt after the rape (Vespa 1984), while other reports seemed to take her side, noting that "her lengthy ordeal on the witness stand was compounded by the unusual legal proceedings" (Starr 1984, 21). Some network stories mentioned that there were two trials and numerous defense attorneys.

These themes in turn could be connected to the valiant efforts of victims who did press charges in spite of the treatment they could expect in court. Mainstream coverage supported the victim in a variety of ways. Indeed, support for the victim was so strong that some media accounts of the trial denounced the defense for attempting a consent strategy (the argument that the woman had consented to whatever sexual activity had occurred). After quoting defense attorney Judith Lindahl's statement that "a truth-telling woman cannot be effectively cross-examined or humiliated" during a rape trial, *New York Times* commentator Sydney Schanberg asserted that "this is, of course, nonsense. A skillful defense lawyer—which Miss Lindahl is—can find something in almost any witness's past that lends itself, through clever distortion, to embarrassment or worse. Although Miss Lindahl, in explaining her role at the trial, in no way sought to justify rape, she did encourage the idea that the presumed victim may be the perpetrator" (Schanberg 1984, A31).

Thus, just as news coverage of the Rideout case had expressed overt support for the concept of marital rape, the argument about a woman's integrity and right to decide whether to engage in sexual activity received equal support. News accounts highlighted the victim's courage in coming forward, her strength in enduring the trial, and even her right to be free from accusations of "deserving" or "asking for" rape: "suppose we applied this reasoning to a different situation—a man being robbed at knifepoint by a mugger. He hands over his cash and watch, and the mugger leaves. Did the man consent? Did he in some way—perhaps by flashing his roll of money in a local bar—encourage the mugger to attack him? Has any lawyer ever tried such a defense in a mugging case?" (Schanberg 1984, A31).

But acceptance of the victim's perspective on the issue of consent and gang rape was accomplished at the expense of other important elements of the reformed, victim-based perspective: feminist criticism of news coverage was transformed into a conflict with the Portuguese community. Benedict's analysis suggests that local New Bedford coverage helped to solidify public sentiment against the victim by playing up the "she deserved it" mentality of community members and by seeming to pit the victim against her own community (Benedict 1992, chapter 4). While *both* groups criticized media coverage, these criticisms were often diverted into a drama between two opposing sides: the story that emerged pitted feminists against the local Portuguese citizens. Numerous stories covered the protests at length, and some of these made little mention of the trial or the specifics of the case. Typical of this transformation of complaints about bias was the CBS coverage:

Young: . . . The case has embittered many in this old whaling town. It has pitted against each other not just the defendants and the woman who says she was their victim, but also the Portuguese immigrant community and supporters of woman's lib.

Elizabeth Bennett (New Bedford Woman's Center): We heard the same old myths that we always hear when—when a woman is—is raped, that she must have asked for it, that she shouldn't have been there, that she must be a prostitute.

Manuel Ferreira (Portuguese Times): Well, I'm not saying they are angels or saints or didn't commit a crime either. This has to be proven on the courts [sic], on the trial. But what we're saying is the fact that too much emphasis was given toward the fact that they're Portuguese. (Rather, 24 February 1984)

In their statements, neither the representative of the *Portuguese Times* nor the woman from the New Bedford Woman's Center asserted that the other group was in any way at fault. In fact, both were implicitly criticizing media coverage. However, the lead-in framed their comments as being "pitted against" each other. In general, although both feminists and Portuguese-American groups protested and sometimes supported opposing positions in the case, the point most frequently emphasized by representatives of the Portuguese-American community was that media coverage was biased. Asked to give an example, a representative of the *Portuguese Times* noted that there had been "people in the press room who clapped . . . when the prosecution rested its case, presented his final argument to the jury," and that when "testimony was presented by police officers, by different witnesses, and—and being reported, it was always 'testimony.' But when one of the defendants testified the newspapers reported that he 'gave his tale,' which suggests that it was less than the truth" (Sawyer, 19 March 1984). Rather than focus on the allegations against the press or the point being made, CBS reporter Diane Sawyer switched to the question of "exactly how you think that factors into the trial itself and to the justice served or not served?" She asserted that "the prosecutor, of course, made the point that he's of Portuguese descent too." In general, media representations of the case demonstrated an inability to be self-critical and deflected direct criticism of their coverage onto the charges of one social group toward another.

Two articles in the *New York Times* illustrate the approach of depicting the arguments of feminist and Portuguese protesters as antagonistic to each other:

A silent, candle-lit protest march several days after the incident drew support from more than 2,500 people from throughout the Northeast.

Support for the coalition [against sexist violence] did not come from all quarters, however. The women say they felt resistance from activists within the Committee for Justice, a group that helped raise bail for the defendants, who are immigrants from the Azores. . . . Miss Melo [Committee for Justice spokesperson] said she and others were afraid the coalition's tactics and the public outcry over the incident had resulted in a "lynch-mob attitude" toward the Portuguese population. Coalition members deny this.

"All along we said we were upset by the violent crime," Miss Melo said. "On the other hand, we felt the case was totally off balance. This case was not totally different from other rapes. What made this attract national attention was that six Portuguese were involved."

Miss Bennett [coalition spokesperson] insists that the coalition's goals are larger than this trial. "It's rape in general," she said. "We don't feel that we are overcapitalizing on this one. It's the media that picked it up. We are just responding." (Rangel 1984b, A10)

"There was guilt by national origin," said Miss Melo, a 37-year-old stitcher in a textile factory. "I am worried that they won't get a fair trial."

Although women's groups were particularly outraged, Miss Melo says they were too emotional. "I believe in women's liberation," she said, "but what I'm doing is defending the right of an immigrant to live in this country without being judged guilty." (Butterfield 1984, A6)

In each example, the contrasts implied or asserted by the reporter are not directly supported by the quotes of Miss Melo. The writers imply that her criticism was directed at feminist protesters and organizers, although the actual quotes indicate that the central criticisms are aimed at the justice system and the media. Again, although some antagonism did exist, none of this coverage accurately described the source or cause of the antagonism, other than by the vague implication that some people supported the defendants while others supported the victim. This oversimplified interpretation of the conflict—that each group's central complaint was with the other—limited the expression of rape reform ideas by deflecting feminist criticism and commentary onto the Portuguese defendants and their community.

News stories did not discuss gang rape as a common or deplorable societal problem: rather, only *this* gang rape was discussed, and it was frequently linked to "Portuguese" attitudes about gender and rape. By focusing on the Portuguese community, news coverage managed almost completely to avoid a discussion of the incidence or cause of gang rape within the larger culture.

The initial furor regarding media coverage was over the airing and publishing of extremely negative and ethnically biased comments about Luso-Americans in New Bedford. The district attorney compiled a list of quotations from the local and national press that included a range of harmful and violent opinions about Luso-Americans. The *Fall River Herald* printed the suggestion that "the city would be better off if its Portuguese residents were sent back across the ocean" ("Memorandum in Support," 1984, 6), and *CBS News* re-aired a call-in comment from a local New Bedford station asserting that "they contribute nothing to this country. They don't understand our ways, nor do they want to understand that this country is not like Portugal." Perhaps more to the point, another caller observed that "they don't try to learn the law of the land. They don't try to become involved in a community" (Kuralt, 1 April 1984).

Defense attorneys also played up the defendants' ethnic makeup by arguing that their clients were treated unfairly by the police at several stages in the investigation. The defense argued that the police were "lying in wait" for Vieira, wanting "another shot at obtaining incriminating statements" ("Reply Memorandum of Joseph Vieira," 1984, 7), and that "Joseph Vieira had no English background, left school in the Azores at age eleven, did not understand even the basic premises of trial and arrest within the criminal justice system, and had an abiding trust and belief in the police department's duty to act in a manner consistent with his best interests. He had a similar belief that police actions were not subject to his objection" ("Reply Memorandum of Joseph Vieira," 1984, 2). Defense attorneys argued that, since Vieira had no knowledge of the system in which he was operating and did not speak fluent English, he could not adequately defend himself, and no attorney had been present at his initial interrogation. The case raised significant questions about how an uneducated, non-English–speaking immigrant could receive adequate justice in the United States. However, these questions were not discussed in any detail in the news coverage. In the absence of a direct discussion of the problems of rendering justice to these marginalized defendants, the comments about their lack of community knowledge implied that it was no surprise that those who didn't know the "law of the land" had found themselves in trouble.

This biased view of the case helped eliminate discussion of rape or of rape law reform from the news coverage, as implicit blame for the rape was placed on "uniquely" Luso-American attitudes toward women and rape. The phrase "gang rape" was used to label this crime, but was seldom discussed as a cultural phenomenon (although statistics since

Amir's 1971 work have indicated the prevalence and significance of gang rape). Victim-hating quotes were attributed to Luso-Americans as if the community were responsible for the attitudes that made the rape possible: a *Newsweek* article reported that the guilty verdicts had escalated the anger of New Bedford Portuguese residents who felt the case had brought out anti-Portuguese feelings. It quoted residents saying the victim "had no business being in a bar. She should have been home with her kids instead of out destroying men's lives!" (Beck and Zabarsky 1984, 39). The crime was traced to traditional attitudes held by a particular American subculture, not to the social or political factors identified by feminists (who see gang rape as the natural result of a culture that dehumanizes and objectifies women and encourages men to think of women as subservient) or by the Portuguese community leaders (who believed this gang rape attracted so much lurid attention because it was committed by Portuguese men):

the demonstrators are wrong. What attracted attention were the circumstances of the rape, not its perpetrators. Nor did the victim embarrass her community. As Judge William Young observed, to have reduced the penalties because she visited a bar would "virtually outlaw an entire gender for the style of their dress, the length of their skirts or their choice to enter a place of public refreshment." Nor does the rape shame the victim. The idea that sexual assault dishonors the victim is a cruel, archaic reading of the crime. The jury had no difficulty distinguishing between the trials of the victim and her assailants. May the crowd learn to do the same. ("The Shame in New Bedford and Dallas," 1984, A26)

After the verdicts were announced, one report noted that "sobs and shrieks" filled the courtroom at news of the convictions, and that defendants' "friends and relatives filled the courtroom with their wailing" (Goldman et al. 1984, 39). By implication, Portuguese supporters of the defendants showed an outmoded attitude in blaming the victim.

Reform Ideas in Mainstream News of *Big Dan's*

Despite the large number of attorneys involved in the two Big Dan's trials, lawyers' comments were sought out much less frequently than in the Rideout case. Feminists, on the other hand, were more frequently and extensively quoted during the New Bedford trials. For the most part, expert commentary was sought not for the trial, nor for ideas about rape or rape law reform, but for the issues *surrounding* the trial. Feminists were occasionally asked to explain the rape shield law (used to eliminate sexual history evidence from this case). In one *CBS Morning News* story, a Pennsylvania judge was interviewed on this subject:

Sawyer: But there are cases, as Betty Ann was saying again, that the defense attorneys were saying that they had a lot of things they couldn't introduce that would have helped their clients, that should have been introduced? *Judge Richette*: Oh, certainly. They can bring in almost anything that they would want in any kind of criminal trial. But we have rules of evidence. And evidence must be relevant. The rape shield laws are based on the principle that a woman's past sexual history, indeed her past life, is not relevant to the issue at trial which is whether or not she was penetrated against her consent. . . . Rape trials used to be horror shows, packed to the gills with onlookers and spectators. We've removed that element and we've tried to make them fair and normalize them as we would any other trial. *Sawyer*: In this case, though, they introduced the fact that the woman had cheated on welfare. They introduced some other evidence that she—she was living with two children that she had had out of wedlock. *Judge Richette*: But Diane, what does that have to do with whether or not these men sexually assaulted her?" (Sawyer, 22 March 1984)

Although the interviewer's attitude is unclear, the rationale for the new rules of evidence was clearly articulated here.

In general, news media showed more willingness to recognize feminist thought on the issue of rape in the Big Dan's trial than it had during the Rideout case. In a *New York Times* article, local feminists were interviewed about their work on the trial: "immediately after the multiple rape, organizers say, the victim was treated in press reports and by the public as a criminal who should have known better than to go into the bar unescorted. 'It made me very angry,' said Melissa Slaughter. . . . 'It reinforced things I always knew were there in the public mind'" (Rangel 1984b, A10). In another report, feminists explained the problems posed when sexual history testimony is accepted as evidence of "character": "this is a perfect case study of what women have to go through in rape trials. . . . She ended up on trial instead of the defendants" (Rangel, 1984c, 22). An ABC story quoted at length from the comments of a rape victim who said she had had to leave the room on the first day of the trial because it was so painful (Jennings, 15 March 1984).

Some acknowledgment was also given to the claim that the televised trial could have a chilling effect on victims who might now be afraid to come forward, having seen firsthand the methods used to discredit victim-witnesses in rape trials. ABC noted estimates that only one in ten victims of rape report it to the police, and that while this statistic had been improving in Massachusetts, this case might create a setback. NBC reported that the testimony was graphic and the defense was "rough," concluding that "sometimes it does seem like the alleged victim is on trial" (Jennings, 29 February 1984). This story also mentioned that the victim had had to face six defense attorneys, and it included a segment of trial interrogation to illustrate the point.

For the most part, however, news coverage of the Big Dan's case followed a familiar scenario: the emphasis on dramatic information failed to include discussions of systems of power, logic, or reasoning. This approach worked to contain the rape reform message, as it had in the coverage of *Rideout*. In addition, during the coverage of both cases, mainstream media expressed support for an important element of the victim's perspective on the reality of rape. Mainstream discussions of the Big Dan's case indicated that rape victims deserved sympathy for several reasons, including the ordeal of the trial they must undergo and the unfair belief that victims ask for rape. But this expression of support was given at the expense of other issues of concern to rape law reformers: feminist criticism of the news coverage was often depicted in conflict with the Portuguese community, and Portuguese Americans were linked with the traditional belief that victims provoke rape.

News Coverage of *Dotson*

While news coverage of the Rideout and Big Dan's cases included open affirmation of key elements of the feminist position on rape and rape law reform, coverage of the Dotson case was more diffuse in its support. Although some articles expressed concern that Webb's recantation would "turn back the clock" and take back hard-earned credibility from the victims of rape, most coverage also reopened questions of how and whether juries could accurately determine the truth in cases of rape. This case is an excellent example of the trend Faludi describes in *Backlash* (1991): once a small degree of change has been accomplished, mainstream news reports a story that illustrates how that change has gone *too far*. In effect, news coverage of the Dotson case delineated the limits of acceptable change in mainstream ideology about rape: here, it seemed, was a woman who did lie about being raped, and an innocent man was imprisoned as a result. Given this substantiation of the time-honored "truth" about rape, women could hardly be believed simply because they convincingly claimed that a rape had occurred. In short, news coverage of this case rejected the notion that uncorroborated testimony could be adequate in some rape cases, reinforcing the traditional view that rape claimants are likely to be liars. Mainstream ideology still held that rape was a special crime with regard to evidence and testimony, and it easily accepted Webb's recantation as support for this idea.

Traditional Ideas about Rape in Mainstream News

Much of the news coverage surrounding the case rekindled the traditional male fears of false accusation and mistaken identification. *U.S. News and World Report* asserted that the case raised "troubling legal questions on the handling of sexual-assault cases" ("Rape: New Controversy on Old Issue," 1985, 52). The *U.S. News* preview of the case captured the tone of much of the retrospective questioning that ensued by asking whether the victim lied and asserting that "a startling confession" furthered "far-ranging concerns over how the law deals with sexual violence" (52). Some articles implicitly questioned the wisdom of rape law reform without openly criticizing statutory revisions. A *Chicago Tribune* article announced in bold print: "Revelations of false charges have brought a change in attitude toward the crime and the 'criminals'" (Swanson 1985, 2.1). The article began by noting that

in March, the case that advocates of rape reform had dreaded broke into the news when Cathy Crowell Webb claimed on national television that she had lied about being raped in 1977. The story would not go away. . . . Rape reform advocates . . . wonder if the tide is changing after a decade or so of progress that has resulted in tougher laws and more compassion for victims. Police and prosecutors wonder when the next Dougan [another recanting case] or Webb will come along and whether they will be able to recognize her. (Swanson 1985, 2.1)

Although a large proportion of the Dotson coverage did not directly address rape law reform issues, an anti-reform slant underscored the tendency of news coverage to promote traditional ideas about rape, especially the "special nature" of rape with regard to the truthfulness of the victim and the ability of the jury to make an accurate judgment. Much of the reporting rearticulated traditional cautions about the special nature of rape in the wake of Webb's recantation. The descriptive logic of headlines such as "Woman Goes Public to Undo Rape 'Lie,'" "'Wronged Man' Gets Court Date" (Kass and Lipinski 1985, 1.1), "Who's Using Whom in Dotson TV Flap?" (Daley 1985, 2.1) and "Who Is the Real Victim?" (Starr and King 1985, 69) reinforced the familiar notion of rape victims as liars.

As with *Rideout*, the victim's character was the central dramatic focus of news coverage. Webb's initial recantation was made with great fanfare and often taken at face value: Webb was retracting her story, therefore the rape had not occurred, and Dotson was innocent. For the first few days after her announcement, news sources ran stories quoting Webb, her attorney, and Dotson's mother and sister that assumed Webb's veracity in recanting the original story. On the first day after the announcement, *CBS Evening News* reported:

Currier: Dotson, now 28, was convicted in 1979 of raping a suburban Chicago teenage girl, who identified him in a police lineup as her attacker. But *the story has unravelled.* The woman, now 23, and the mother of two children, signed a confession stating she lied about the rape charge to cover up a sexual experience with another man, which she feared might have led to pregnancy. *John McLario (woman's attorney):* It was a lie and it just kept progressing and growing and she felt that she could not withdraw from the lie. (Currier, 27 March 1985; emphasis added)

Two weeks later, *CBS News* again accepted Webb's word even after Judge Samuel's decision:

Kurtis: Convicted rapist Gary Dotson was sent back to prison by a Cook County, Illinois circuit judge even after his accuser, Cathleen Crowell Webb, recanted her testimony. Webb later told ABC News [sic] why she waited six years to try to clear Dotson. *Webb*: Prior to my decision to become a Christian three-and-a-half years ago, I didn't have a soft conscience about this. I—I hardened my conscience and tried to forget what I had done. (Kurtis, 12 April 1985)

Many reports placed the presumption of truth with the new story rather than with the original version. The *New York Times'* initial report quoted Webb extensively in explaining her actions, including her report that she had invented the rape because she feared pregnancy after having had sex with her boyfriend. This article excerpted Webb's affidavit, noting her claim that she had ripped her clothes and scratched and bruised herself to fake the rape. Finally, the article stated that "Miss Crowell later gave the police a general description of the *nonexistent attacker*" ("Woman Recants a Rape Charge Six Years Later," 1985, L6; emphasis added). Six early network television stories outlined Webb's rationale for making up this "lie." Only later, during Governor James Thompson's clemency hearing, did news stories begin to question these claims.

Dramatic early reporting in the case often simply assumed the veracity of Webb's recantation. Later, when contradictions in her testimony emerged, many stories questioned her "veracity" and concluded that she had to have been lying at one time or another. Both approaches fit the traditional framework. Meanwhile, larger questions about rape, rapists, and rape victims were raised only briefly and infrequently and even then merely drew upon the old myths. Media coverage implicitly questioned changes in social and legal attitudes and values, even when they explicitly supported the goals of rape law reform: "twenty years ago, jurors and police tended to have grave doubts about the testimony of rape victims. Then the pendulum started to swing the other way. This case may produce a healthy skepticism about the testimony of both parties" (A. Dershowitz quoted in "Rape: New Controversy on Old Issues," 1985, 52). Another piece made references to "the enigmatic Cathleen Webb" (Daley 1985).

In 1985, news coverage focused primarily on discrediting Webb. This was much like the tactic used by John Rideout's attorney: establish that the complainant "lacks veracity," and you cast doubt on any story she tells. *CBS Morning News* reported before the hearing that Judge Samuels would rule on "whether the rape was real or imagined" (Kurtis, 5 April 1985). Many reporters seemed confused by Webb's conflicting stories, able only to conclude that "we don't know if Cathy Webb has the truth in her" and that "justice is a messy business. So is rape and so is deceit" (Daley 1985, 2.1). A *Chicago Tribune* article noted that "Webb's credibility as a witness was crucial, for it was that—not whether Dotson was guilty or innocent—that framed the narrow issue of perjury brought before the court by Warren Lupel, Dotson's attorney" (Kass and Lipinski 1985, 1.1).

News magazines such as *Time* and *Newsweek*, in addition to popular magazines such as *People*, raised questions about the history of rape law reform—questions that had already been decided in the legal arena. *Newsweek*'s comment that "after a long-overdue national consciousness-raising has rejected the traditions of the Common Law, [Webb was] living proof that sometimes a 'rape victim' can't be trusted after all" (Press et al. 1985, 60) suggested that perhaps rape cases *should* still be considered special. In general, hints that rape deserved status as a special crime were based on suggestions that Webb's credibility was destroyed by her recantation, no matter which of her stories were true. ABC quoted attorney Alan Dershowitz at length:

the judge was certainly following established law by refusing to accept recanted testimony. Look, nobody can know for sure which time she was lying. We can all agree that she lied once under oath and she did it quite convincingly . . . nobody can satisfy the burden of proof when you have a witness who is an admitted liar and who may have been lying then and who may be lying now. . . . A second jury would hear a witness who has a history of lying at least once. (Jennings, 12 April 1985)

A *Newsweek* article reminded readers that rape had always held "special case" status in the eyes of the law. The article referred to the Dotson case as having the elements of a "classic legal nightmare": a confused teenager accuses an innocent man, he is convicted and receives a long sentence based on her testimony (Starr and King 1985, 69). ABC reported that "historically, recanted testimony rarely leads to reversal of a judge's verdict, but many legal experts think this case was extraordinary." The story included comments from an attorney who said that "it seems unconscionable to keep somebody in prison when the sole witness against him says 'I was lying' " (Jennings, 12 April 1985).

The human drama surrounding the highly publicized retraction easily lent itself to emotional coverage: immediately following Webb's recantation Dotson was released on bond; after an initial hearing he was sent back to prison; and he was eventually freed after Governor James Thompson conducted a special clemency hearing. One report noted that "supporters on the street" could not comprehend "why a judge would not take the word of the victim . . . who now says she was never raped by

Dotson or anyone" (Kurtis, 15 April 1985). Another noted that a legal expert had "testified in favor of a full pardon for Mr. Dotson, a position clearly endorsed by many of the people who have been attending the hearing" (Shipp 1985b). Citizens were quoted in their determination to "keep working" and "not . . . let this thing rest" (Kurtis, 12 April 1985).

It would have been difficult not to want Dotson freed after reading or watching news coverage of the case. The media depictions of Dotson as being entirely without malice toward Webb (who by implication had greatly wronged him) rendered him, like John Rideout, an unlikely rapist. In the mainstream media, Dotson's "new" character went a long way toward suggesting his innocence. Dotson was portrayed as a sympathetic character who enjoyed a good joke or prank but who was not in the least malicious or violent.

Reports of Dotson's youth depicted him as a harmless, happy-go-lucky individual who was "involved with various kinds of mischief and petty thefts" (Starr and King 1985, 69). In a *Today Show* appearance, attorney John McLario noted that Dotson showed the character of a mischievous young man but not of a rapist, and Jane Pauley asked Dotson whether people would be less suspicious of him if he had been more angry or bitter (Pauley, 15 May 1985). This kind of portrayal, combined with an emphasis on Dotson's forgiving nature, suggested that he was a good and humble person patiently awaiting a decision on his fate. Such coverage reinforced the traditional myth of the stranger rapist: Dotson was not violent, aggressive, or hostile and was becoming more and more familiar to the public. A report of his performance during the governor's hearing gave him high marks for "low-key, unaffected responses" that "frequently evoked laughter" (Starr and King 1985, 69), and Webb asserted on the *Today Show* that "he's not a rapist, he doesn't have the character of a rapist" (Pauley, 15 May 1985). *Time*, after including this same statement, observed that "the painfully inarticulate Dotson insisted he was not angry, that he bore more ill will against the system than against his accuser" (Serrill 1985, 66).

For the purposes of this analysis, the actual innocence or guilt of Gary Dotson is only of marginal importance. It is possible, given the facts of the case, that Webb identified the wrong man. The revised DNA analysis of 1989 indicates that this is indeed what happened, and the facts corroborating that a rape had occurred were stronger than the evidence that Dotson was the rapist. More significant is the way in which the case and the evidence were framed. Once again, the facts of the case fit into the structure of the traditional understanding of rape: to the extent that Dotson was not a violent stranger, he did not have the "character" of a rapist. And throughout news coverage of this case, the implicit understanding of rape as a "special case" crime underlay the fear of wrongful accusation. What emerged from news coverage was the idea that a man might have been wrongly jailed based only on the testimony of the principal witness. If women *were* liars and did have motivations for lying that were related to their sexuality and fear of discovery, then there might still be salient reasons to offer special protections for male defendants.

News accounts were also personalized through frequent references to Dotson's devoted family. Dotson's mother was visible throughout the unfolding of events and was quoted in more than a dozen national news stories. Webb's foster mother was also quoted on numerous occasions. The participants in this strange case formed a fairly unified front: the attorneys for both sides, the victim and convicted rapist, and the families of each were all agreed that Dotson was innocent and should go free. Nearly all the news stories included quotes from one or more of these people, and sources outside this group were seldom quoted.

Dotson's mother Barbara emerged as a central figure, appearing to support her son in every way possible. A *Redbook* story included interviews with both Barbara Dotson and Carol Smith, Webb's foster mother. Mrs. Dotson outlined Gary's brushes with the law and his rebellious teenage years but asserted that "he was basically a sweet boy who always helped out" (Black and Black 1985, 151). *CBS News* quoted her claim that "he's an innocent boy and he wasn't supposed to be put there in the first place. And this girl's come forward and we believe what she's saying" (Kurtis, 12 April 1985). Descriptions of Dotson's mother and sisters and Webb leaving the courtroom in tears helped to intensify the emotional drama of the case. In the initial *New York Times* report, Dotson's mother was quoted as saying she wasn't angry with Webb but grateful because "God came to her and moved her somehow. I think it's encouraging, and Gary feels the same way" ("Woman Recants a Rape Charge Six Years Later," 1985, L6). Several network accounts replayed a television appearance in which a tearful Webb begged forgiveness of Mrs. Dotson. News stories reported that Barbara Dotson personally delivered the check that released her son on bond, and others reported that during his brief freedom Dotson celebrated at home with champagne and pizza while a sign outside announced that Gary Dotson was innocent and was loved and supported by his family. The focus on Dotson and his family diverted attention away from the evidence that pointed strongly to the fact that Webb had been raped, whether by Dotson or someone else.

Many stories suggested that Dotson was being victimized by both Webb and the criminal justice system. *CBS News* included a woman's observation that "the judge just let him out for that week just to tease him" (Kurtis, 12 April 1985). Earlier, *CBS News* had reported that "for the last six miserable years of his life in the Joliet, Illinois prison, Gary Dotson has maintained his innocence in a crime nearly everyone agrees never happened" (Kurtis, 27 March 1985). News stories expressed confusion about legal reasoning that could send a man back to prison even after his accuser recanted. One observer in this case asserted flatly: "forget all the tedious citing of legal precedence and the case history of Illinois law. . . . The judge simply decided not to believe Cathleen the recanter over Cathleen the rape victim" (Granger 1985, 2.1). Without reference to the evidence or legal reasoning in the original trial, such commentary suggested the court had been arbitrary in its decision. The legal decision to deny credibility to Webb's recantation was thus rendered mysterious and lacking in logic or coherence.

Legal reasoning was not only left unexplained but in some cases made to seem arbitrary. *CBS News* ran this story on the case:

Rather: In Markham, Illinois today, a judge upheld the conviction of a 28-year-old man who served six years in prison for a rape his accuser now says never happened. Frank Currier reports. (Shouting in courtroom). *Frank Currier:* Cathleen Webb, a 23-year-old New Hampshire housewife, emerged from the courthouse sobbing, insisting the man she accused of rape eight years ago is innocent. But Gary Eugene Dotson must return to prison, a surprise decision by a judge who did not believe Webb's recanted testimony, an invented rape, she had claimed, to conceal a feared pregnancy after an affair with a boyfriend. After day-long testimony fraught with contradictions, where Dotson himself was unsure of his exact whereabouts the night of the crime, Judge Richard Samuels ruled that Dotson failed to sustain the burden of proof. "I really don't know," he said, "for what unfathomable reason Cathy recanted." Dotson covered his face, and his mother and sisters were led sobbing from the courtroom. Reaction was swift. *Warren Lupel (Dotson's attorney):* I will not abandon him because this is an innocent man in jail, and it's a horrible situation. And I'm gonna do everything I can to get him out. *Currier:* Dotson's last words before preparing to return to prison tonight, "Tell Cathy I forgive her." (11 April 1985)

This story captures the tenor of the media's skepticism toward legal proceedings in the case and its tendency to make no effort to explain legal reasoning: the resulting assumption is that when a rape victim recants, she must have been lying when she made the original accusation. This was especially true in early stories of the case. Later, as Governor Thompson's clemency hearing publicly aired the evidence, numerous stories outlined the evidence that had led to Dotson's conviction. Webb could not explain the letters scratched on her stomach the night of the rape, and her former boyfriend testified that they had not completed intercourse that night, thus contradicting her claim that she feared pregnancy (Jennings, 9 May 1985).

The most frequently quoted experts were attorneys John McLario and Warren Lupel. McLario lent credibility to Webb's lie detector test and made several TV appearances. Lupel was quoted in nine of the thirty-four *CBS News* stories. Warren Lupel wondered, "what does a jury do when a 16-year-old girl who has been brutalized says 'that's the man'?" ("Woman Recants Rape Charge Six Years Later," 1985, L6). Both attorneys made repeated assertions that Dotson was innocent and that he would be vindicated through the hearings. Lupel explained the original verdict by asserting that "in hindsight I can say the jury didn't review the evidence well. They ignored all testimony but hers." He added that the witnesses had been "young, long-haired kids" (ibid).

To further mystify the legal procedures, outside lawyers were asked to comment on recantations in the context of Webb's new story. Sam Adam, "one of Chicago's most prominent criminal defense lawyers," was quoted as saying: "The law has made an ass out of itself and the judge has helped it out, if you want to know the truth" ("Amid Outcry and Debate Over Judge's Decision, Man Resumes His Term for Rape," 1985, 1). Adam, asserting that this recantation was different from precedents cited by Samuels in his decision to send Dotson back to prison, commented further that "this situation is outside the recanting cases and has nothing to do with them," thereby implying that with respect to the law rape cases were unique.

Rape Reform Ideas in News Coverage of *Dotson*

Although much coverage surrounding this case favored the traditional male perspective on rape (fears of false accusation and mistaken identity, rape treated as unique with respect to the law because of the "likelihood" of frivolous claims), reform views were articulated in several ways. First, some attorneys and judges (those who later wrote law review essays on the case) believed strongly that Webb's original story was the true story. Attorney Margaret Frossard explained with regard to Webb's original testimony, "I was of the mindset that she was telling the truth. . . . My gut reaction was that she was telling the truth" (Lipinski 1985, 2.1). Next, some stories outlined the contradictory evidence given by Webb *in recanting*, indicating that the case was more complicated than a simple change of heart due to a guilty conscience. Several news stories traced the inconsistencies between Webb's recantation and the physical evidence presented at the original trial; inconsistencies between Dotson's story and the testimony of his alibi witnesses were also noted. NBC reported that one of Dotson's alibi witnesses claimed they had been watching *The Love Boat* at the time of the rape, but a network representative testified that *The Love Boat* did not air until several months later (Brokaw, 17 May 1985). Another network account expressed doubts about Webb's recantation and noted that Dotson's "own alibi witnesses contradicted him in court" (Jennings, 12 April 1985).

These enumerations of the points of inconsistency gave a fairly clear picture of how testimony, including victim testimony about rape, could be evaluated by attorneys and judges (Shipp 1985b; Lipinski 1985). Many other articles focused on the testimony of one or two parties who contradicted Webb's recanted version (see Shipp 1985c; Shipp 1985a). However, references to the prosecution's claim that a young girl simply could not fake a rape so convincingly and their questions as to whether Webb's new faith prevented her from judging another person were extremely rare (Rather, 11 May 1985; Brokaw, 12 April 1985).

Ironically, although this case included bizarre and atypical elements in comparison to other rape trials, it also evoked some of the most direct discussion of law reform of any of the three cases. *Newsweek* devoted an entire five-page article to the history and efforts of law reform, and numerous articles noted that this case could have a chilling effect on future rape victims who might be afraid to come forward because they would be considered liars (Press et al. 1985). These articles also quoted feminists on the issue of veracity. *Newsweek*'s lengthy treatment of reform efforts quoted Susan Estrich: "The whole effort at reforming rape laws has been an attack on the premise that women who bring complaints are suspect. There's no proof whatsoever that rape complaints are more unfounded than those of any other crimes. Now Webb will be used to lend credence to all the fundamentally sexist assumptions about women" (Press et al. 1985, 61).

Out of the thirty-four CBS stories, only one discussion of rape law reform was included. Three interviewees identified as a rape victim, a psychologist, and a law professor were asked for comments on the possible effects of the case:

Lucinda [victim]: "One of the common stereotypes is that women lie and—don't get raped, and I'm very concerned about that, you know, women aren't going to be believed anymore. I—I think that that would be a horrible repercussion of this case. . . ." *Paul Rothstein [law professor]:* "I think you put your finger right on it. This is going to turn the clock back on a long, hard-fought effort over the past 15 years to bring the law's attitude about rape and sex crimes out of the 16th century into the modern day. The law, until about 15 years ago, didn't believe any rape victims." (Kuralt 19 May 1985)

Thus, despite some discussions of the history of rape law reform and the progress made by reformers that emerged in the coverage of the case, much of the information was undercut: highly dramatic and personalized coverage, which focused on Webb's lack of veracity and Dotson's affable character and strong family relationships, eliminated almost all analysis of rape per se. In addition, the high-profile attorneys and participants in this case provided plenty of dramatic and personalized information to fill news stories; moreover, all of them asserted that the victim had been lying when she testified that Dotson had raped her in 1977. All those quoted with any frequency implied or asserted that Webb had been able to fool a jury, judge, parents, police officers, and medical examiner in claiming that she had been raped. These quotes served to divert attention away from evidence that a rape had been committed, and away from an interrogation of Webb's motives for recanting the entire story rather than only her identification of Dotson.

Conclusion

News coverage of these three trials functioned as a sort of ideological gatekeeper in the give-and-take process of social change. While many of the elements that define news reportage also served to disadvantage, limit, or eliminate discussion of reformed ideas, news coverage of these trials also outlined where and how these ideas were being accepted into mainstream ideology. During the Rideout case, news reports expressed overt recognition of the problem of marital rape while revealing an underlying uneasiness about how the new Oregon law could be interpreted. During the Big Dan's case, reports supported the feminist notion that rape trials are unfair to victims, who do not deserve or ask for brutal gang rape, but also suggested that only the Portuguese-American community held the attitudes that perpetuated or led to the attack. Reports of the Dotson case primarily expressed the limitation on the acceptance of further reform ideas into the dominant ideology about rape: women could lie about rape and fool a jury, and therefore male fears about false accusation were not unfounded. If men were being falsely imprisoned, then perhaps the ideas behind rape law reform were incorrect and had been rashly accepted into law.

Although none of these cases was significant from a legal perspective, they received more national media attention than any other rape trial between 1974 and 1987. Coverage of each of these cases followed the pattern described at the beginning of this chapter: compelling personal information, particularly testimony concerning the victim's character, provided the substance of the coverage; news stories seldom described legal history or trial strategy, which could have explained relevant testimony and its impact on the verdict; and trial attorneys were by far the most frequently consulted "experts." Most important, these stories were not about rape law reform, but about the people embroiled in particular cases. Dramatic appeal was drawn from both testimony and case characteristics that fit into the old model for understanding rape. Elements such as a lying victim, false accusations, and sexual history evidence repeatedly made headlines and were the focus of news commentary. Finally, the victims, in every case, were judged according to traditional criteria: Greta Rideout, portrayed as a lying, manipulative and confused woman, was openly ridiculed until after the trial verdict was delivered; the Big Dan's victim was portrayed as a youthful "mother of two"; and Cathleen Crowell Webb, described primarily as a liar, was believed implicitly when she recanted.

Each of these cases also saw the perpetrators molded to fit traditional character types. Greta Rideout was portrayed as the classic manipulating woman who was smarter than her husband and not afraid to use threats, false accusations, and lies to fulfill her desires for sex, fame, and fortune. John Rideout was depicted as a young, sincere, and traditional man who was not malicious or even clever. The Big Dan's rapists came across as brutal men who did not even think that what they had done was a crime. Gary Dotson was portrayed as an agreeable and forgiving man who simply wanted his freedom. In each case media coverage implicitly and explicitly validated elements of the traditional understanding of rape.

While rape law reform activities put these cases on the national agenda, coherent, widely circulated ideas about the concepts central to rape law reform were largely unavailable to help the public make sense of these cases. In general, mainstream news coverage of these trials was not a source for meaningful explanations of social reform initiatives, tending instead to cover trial-related issues at the expense of larger sense-making frameworks. In addition, the public was given a paltry analysis of legal reasoning and how it fit within the framework of an effort for social change. In its penchant for case-specific facts, the news media seldom discussed the larger social issues or problems, such as relations of power and gender, that created the conditions for the verdicts in the respective cases. However, some limited reform messages were included in discussions of each case, in addition to the key reform elements presented in the bulk of mainstream coverage. This was accomplished primarily through the commentary of rape reformers, and secondarily through trial attorneys who sometimes used rape reform ideas to argue their cases.

Note

1. During the period of these trials, knowledge of what is now known as battered wife syndrome was emerging in a few feminist and sociology texts (see *Victimology* [special issue; v. 2.3–2.4, 1977–1978]). However, this knowledge did not enjoy a wider social legitimacy.

Chapter 5
Popular Re-Presentations

The Burning Bed, a television film based on a case in which a woman kills her battering husband, is one of several fictional treatments that have been instrumental in bringing social issues to the attention of a wide audience. Elayne Rapping has observed that such movies-of-the-week are often "presented as socially important documents, on the cutting edge of public debate, and, in fact, a focal point for engaging us, as a nation, in a much larger public sphere" (Rapping 1992, xi). Although not all the texts examined here are movies-of-the-week, they all performed a function similar to the one Rapping describes. The four fictionalized treatments of the rape cases under examination (both a made-for-TV movie and a Hollywood film were based on the Big Dan's case) helped to keep rape law reform issues in the national spotlight. Yet, as with news coverage, generic constraints of popular genres shaped and contained the messages of these movies.

The fictionalized versions of these cases selected and expanded on important news themes while at the same time elaborating new elements not found in most mainstream coverage. Fiction constrained the expression of rape reform ideas, but in a different and less complete way than did mainstream news. As Fiske has noted, news and fiction are "modalities" of each other (Fiske 1989). In large part, the dramatic and highly personalized nature of news coverage is even further exaggerated in fictional treatments, where dramatic narrative and personal conflict are even more central, and where the need for "expert" validation and "objective" balance is less salient. In effect, fiction is even more personalized than news in that it must portray complex characters rather than the one-dimensional stereotypes news sources often rely upon. In the fictional versions of these cases, the complexity of the victims' characters led to a more sympathetic understanding of their experiences than that found in news coverage. These texts relied more heavily on dramatic content than did the news reports, with the result that the motivations, feelings, and experiences of the female victims were emphasized and legitimated.

This chapter examines the post-trial portrayals of the Rideout, Big Dan's, and Dotson cases and argues that each existed as a modality of news but also as a sort of second phase in the complex process through which rape law reform ideas were accepted into mainstream ideology and discourse. In this second phase of negotiation between the dominant and challenging ideologies, there was more room for the articulation of reform views than in the first (news coverage) phase. Thus, whereas the complexity of a coherent feminist view was absent from news coverage of all three cases, two of the fictionalized versions articulated a coherent feminist perspective by focusing on the victim as protagonist, while a third legitimated the victim's perspective through an emphasis on female solidarity. In a way, it seems as if the news prepared the way for these fictionalized portrayals by selecting elements that could be adapted or appropriated into the dominant ideology. In *Rape and Marriage: The Rideout Case* and *The Accused*, the victim's perspective is privileged, and both victims defend their positions against traditional views about rape. Although the victim in *Silent Witness* has a small part and commits suicide before the end of the trial, this version of the Big Dan's case, like the news coverage, focused in part on the idea that even a victim with "low credibility" does not deserve or ask for gang rape.

Once mainstream news coverage of these cases prepared the ground, the fictionalized portrayals moved a step further in articulating and legitimizing the victim's perspective on their experiences. *Rape and Marriage: The Rideout Case, The Accused,* and *Silent Witness* portray victims with legitimate fears, experiences, and concerns. The Rideout TV movie depicts John Rideout raping Greta; *The Accused* depicts a poor, sexually active, drug-using victim who refuses to compromise her reputation to an outmoded view of female sexuality. *Silent Witness* portrays an alcoholic victim who commits suicide under the strain of the trial, leaving a sympathetic female witness to demand justice in her place. *Forgive Me,* Cathleen Webb's autobiographical book about the Dotson case, serves as an ideological endpoint, reinforcing traditional myths about rape by illustrating that women can easily fake rape and thus warning that the progress of rape law reform could go too far.

Popular representations also add to the treatment of rape cases new elements that are not part of news coverage. Fiction is able to include more peripheral characters as part of the story, so it is not constrained to the key players in the trial itself. Likewise, fiction is freer to determine the time frame in which the story takes place and is not required to start with the crime and end with the acquittal or conviction of the defendant. Thus, all four fictionalized portrayals begin well before the actual trial, suggesting explanations and motivations for events before they happen. Although news coverage did provide some background reports on the cases (for example, to describe the Rideouts' home life), the historical framework was haphazardly presented. Perhaps more important, the fictionalized versions also often included a female point of view.

The use of perspective further enables sympathetic characterizations of the victims. These fictionalized treatments all present a clearly articulated and well-developed point of view for the female victim: each presents a "common woman's voice." While the trials serve as important focal points in these texts, other elements and periods of the women's lives prove to be equally important.

While the development of a point of view is important in conveying a coherent explanation of the motivations and experiences of rape victims, fictionalized recreations also inhibit the dissemination of the messages of rape law reformers. The hegemonic power of mass-circulation, fictionalized texts works against social change: ideology works by "*masking, displacing,* and *naturalizing* social problems and contradictions" (Goodwin and Whannel 1990, 96, emphasis in original). Although Goodwin and Whannel here refer to television, mainstream popular genres, in any medium, can be said to mask, displace, and naturalize social problems and contradictions (see Radway 1984; Fiske 1989). Just as mainstream news coverage elided many feminist ideas about rape and rape law reform in its interpretations of these cases, so too do the fictionalized versions perform the work of ideological maintenance. In the fictionalized texts the characters, their stories, and the accompanying problems and tensions are presented in personal or interpersonal terms rather that in generalized, social terms. In other words, the exigencies of a tightly controlled plot are at odds with the full expression of a political message, and each story stops short of suggesting radical changes in power structures or cultural practices. Nevertheless, two of the four fictionalized treatments analyzed here (*Rape and Marriage* and *The Accused*) articulate basic elements of rape law reform.

Rape and Marriage: The Rideout Case

Elayne Rapping's 1992 book on the TV movie-of-the-week argues for its significance in bringing personal and feminist issues into the public sphere. In *The Movie of the Week: Private Stories, Public Events,* she notes that "the genre is a discursive site upon which conflicts and contradictions inherent in the existence of the family as an institution within bourgeois society are worked out. Oppositional polarities between matters of privacy and political interventions, marital harmony and gender conflict" are depicted while at the same time "incorporating oppositional voices and concerns" (Rapping 1992, xl). Rapping discusses the ability of this genre to both allow for the articulation of social change messages and to constrain and limit this expression, noting both that they move "inexorably toward the obligatory 'happy ending, nice and tidy,'" and that they are "in their own quiet, contradictory ways, more than somewhat subversive of existing attitudes about sex, marriage, and the family" (Rapping 1992, 69). According to Rapping, then, the television movie-of-the-week does provide a space for the expression of oppositional ideas and perspectives, especially as they relate to the experiences of women within the patriarchal institutions of marriage and family. Yet this function is balanced by an opposing phenomenon: the narratives allow women to allay fears through the reinforcement of those same institutions. These movies have a "common concern with the irreconcilable contradictions faced by modern women" but stop short of suggesting radical alterations of structures of gender and power (Rapping 1992, 100). All of the fictionalized texts examined here deal with such contradictions, but none provides solutions outside the traditional patriarchal institutions. Two of these texts are TV movies and as such support Rapping's observations most clearly.

The CBS movie-of-the-week based on the Rideout case aired a year and a half after the end of the trial. It told the story of both the alleged rape and the subsequent trial primarily from Greta's perspective. The film was structured as a romance, opening with Greta and John embracing in their car at the beach and remembering the times before their daughter was born and before John's employment problems. The story develops as Greta files charges against John for rape, and the Rideouts are separated from each other by the authorities. John's cause is taken up by a successful Salem defense attorney, while Greta is given advice and housing by women from a rape crisis center. Both John's attorneys and the women's crisis center workers are depicted as people with clear perspectives and goals, willing to use the Rideout case to obtain something for their own benefit. The attorneys seek prestige and vindication of their opinion that the new rape law is unfair to men, and the feminists seek a test case to prove the validity of the new law and to provide an example for other battered women. Each of the Rideouts seems to be a pawn in a larger game being played by these groups, a game the young couple cannot understand or effectively resist. Both Rideouts are shown asking about their spouses and expressing a desire to be back together: at one point Greta says she is tired of fighting and just wants to be at home with John. Meanwhile, John is shown requesting that his attorney not hurt Greta during the trial. In one way, the story that unfolds in the film is the story of a young couple separated by forces beyond their control; their mutual desire is to get back together and resume their normal lives.

Like the news coverage, *Rape and Marriage: The Rideout Case* portrays the Rideouts as a naive and confused couple. Greta, incredulous at seeing the defense attorney and district attorney on speaking terms, comments, "I thought they were enemies,"[1] and John seems not to understand that his situation is serious, telling his attorney that he wants to "just talk to Greta" and "work things out." Themes of naivete and joint victimization that were present in news coverage become even more central in the television film, where the idea that the two are caught up in events they cannot understand or control is dominant. Their plight is presented, in part, as a joint predicament: both attorneys and feminist volunteers become obstacles to the resolution of the romance narrative; only after the trial are Greta and John able to overcome these obstacles to be reunited. At the end of the film, the Rideouts are depicted embracing in their car, back together after their lengthy legal ordeal. Although the film includes an epilogue stating that the Rideouts eventually separated for good, the final shot ends with them together, embracing after the trial.

In *Rape and Marriage*, the romanticization of the relationship between Greta and John serves to mask contradictions between necessarily conflicting interpretations of the event in question. The film emphasizes both the joint victimization of Greta and John as low-class pawns of the better educated and more sophisticated feminists and defense attorney, while at the same time focusing on the reality of John's victimization of Greta. Greta comments to John in the final scene, "I think we're the only ones who know how awful it was . . . the trial and everything." The questions of who can rape, who can be raped, and what constitutes rape are raised but remain peripheral to the requirements of the narrative. Echoing a common news theme, John is portrayed as a simple person with little comprehension of the workings of the court or of his own marriage, hardly a vicious criminal. Likewise, although a feminist perspective is clearly articulated by feminist characters and through a focus on Greta's point of view, feminists and their principles are peripheral to the romance narrative. This story develops without resolving questions about troubled and violent marital relationships, the role of law within families, and institutionalized problems of unemployment and gendered work. The television film version relies on an "us against them" perspective, which forces Greta and John closer together while eliding issues of problematic gender relations.

This movie-of-the-week also fits Rapping's definition by incorporating a good deal of oppositional discourse into the highly structured narrative, albeit in a contradictory way. Although a few scenes from John's perspective are included, the film for the most part takes on Greta's perspective. Most important, the day of the alleged rape is shown three times. In the first rendition, which is presented as the objective view of what really happened, the rape is not shown, but is represented by a close-up of the closed door of the Rideout apartment. Events leading up to the alleged rape are portrayed in detail, including close-ups of Greta hiding, watching John tamper with her car, and running away. Then, during the trial, the events leading up to the incident are re-presented twice. The version shown during Greta's testimony incorporates footage very similar to (and in some shots identical to) the initial version, with the addition of Greta's version of the actual rape. The second account, representing John's story, uses different footage and adds John's version of consensual intercourse, strongly implying that John is lying and that Greta is telling the truth. In addition, the original version includes frightening music and focuses on Greta's worried attempts to hide from John. After the rape Greta is shown running frantically to a neighbor's house to hide under the kitchen counter and telephone the police and the crisis center.

Greta's perspective is also represented when the testimony of friendly witnesses is used against her under the district attorney's unenthusiastic and inadequate prosecution of the case. The testimony of Greta's friend, who clearly wishes to state that Greta is basically honest, is misrepresented by the skilled defense attorney as an outright admission that she is a liar on matters of sex. The feminist rape crisis workers criticize District Attorney Gortmaker for scuttling the case for political reasons; in several scenes they question the makeup of the jury, the D.A.'s motivation in refusing to reduce the charges to gain a conviction on a lesser charge, and the "old boy" network at the courthouse. Thus, the film depicts a variety of factors that make it difficult for Greta to fully articulate her position and experience in court.

The legitimacy afforded the victim's experience offers a view of marital rape that was not available in news coverage of the case. The dramatic music and long shots of John chasing Greta through the park help viewers experience her fear, as does her trembling call to the police from under her neighbor's kitchen counter. In addition, prolonged attention is given to John's search for Greta, his tampering with her car, her desperate attempts to hide, and to John's growing anger at being unable to find her. This dimension of the reality of Greta's fear was almost entirely absent from news coverage of the case. The film's story is based on the assumption that Greta had really "gone through something" and that she needed help and support to recover from it. She is portrayed as honest, naive, and earnestly striving for self-improvement. In presenting Greta's perspective in a coherent and sympathetic way, the television movie offers a more multi-dimensional characterization of Greta and suggests that one person could be strong, confused, promiscuous, prone to fantasies, and also a victim of rape.[2]

The television film version further develops Greta's perspective by including her lengthy testimony as to the amount and type of resistance she was able to offer—testimony that was only rarely included in the news coverage. In the television portrayal, Greta asserts that she refused to touch John until he threatened to punch her again if she did not. The fictionalized version includes much more detail regarding this testimony on forcible compulsion. Greta's version of the rape, particularly her effort to resist, is vividly depicted: "I was trying to get John's hands off my throat. . . . I couldn't breathe. . . . I almost fainted. . . . He then took a closed fist with his right hand and slammed down on my face, almost knocking me out. I had at that point decided to submit to him, to what he wanted. My jaw hurt. I thought I'd have a broken jaw if I was hit any more." In the television film, a relatively large proportion of attention is given to the question of resistance, with Greta emphasizing several times that John threatened to hit the other side of her face if she didn't comply. Several aspects of the news coverage are also present in the movie: The fictionalized Charles Burt makes the same accusation as the real Charles Burt did; a sign in the crisis center clearly reads "If she says no! It's rape"; and Greta is heard repeating those words to John later that day (clearly establishing in the film that she got her definition from the women's center). But Greta is also shown giving her own story of how her experiences fit the accepted definition of rape. Through her description, the film includes a clear definition of what "forcible compulsion" should mean. This contrasts sharply with the mainstream news reports' waffling on the questions of how to define marital rape and how to judge Greta's word against John's.

Yet the television movie creates its own set of contradictions by attempting to present the events primarily, and sympathetically, from Greta's viewpoint but at the same time offering only fragmented answers to questions about the problems of marital violence and rape. In taking Greta's point of view, it includes a series of scenes where she interacts with the women from the rape crisis center. These feminists are portrayed as pushy and opinionated but committed to helping women like Greta who are caught in violent relationships. The scenes with the crisis center workers articulate feminist ideas about marriage, battering, and rape. For example, during Greta's first visit to the center, she explains that the "fights are awful . . . and they're getting worse." Greta describes a pattern of escalation in which she becomes increasingly afraid of John.

In a later conversation, Greta and a counselor agree that being caught in a violent relationship is like being addicted to drugs. Greta admits "I guess I'm hooked." The counselor, Helen, discusses patterns of victimization that are difficult to change, noting that "being a victim is a hard habit to break." Helen mentions more than once that she had two marriages to violent men, but that she was able to pull through by leaving them. Later, in Greta's kitchen, Helen wonders why battered women keep going back to their men, and then remembers, "I do understand. . . . I was there once, where you are . . . I'm just so far away from it now," suggesting that it is possible to get away permanently. In this scene, Helen also alludes to the scope of the problem, asserting that "we see hundreds of women just like you." Unlike the news coverage, these exchanges assume that Greta's accusation is not false, that Greta was raped by her husband, and that it is possible to tell the difference between a violent and abusive relationship and a "little slapping and shoving" or a "marital tiff."

Rape and Marriage: The Rideout Case does not fully endorse or embrace this feminist position: it depicts the crisis center volunteers as overly domineering, repeatedly pushing Greta toward the next step in the prosecution. The Women's Crisis Center emerges as a significant force in urging Greta to press charges against John: First, Helen suggests to Greta that she call the police. Second, the defense attorney asserts that Greta had only learned about the feminist definition of rape from the crisis center, after the aforementioned sign is clearly shown in the crisis center window. Third, Helen accompanies Greta to the police station, asserting that "Greta was raped! She was beaten into submission!," and "we . . . she wants to press charges NOW."

The film tempers the victim's perspective, depicting Greta more as a pawn than as someone with personal knowledge and a resulting desire for justice. The fictional Helen's overbearing manner and the almost religious commitment of the crisis center women are seen as the primary reasons the case goes to trial. It is Helen who first suggests that Greta press charges for rape rather than assault (which the police recommend), and Helen assures Greta that she would be an example to other women because of her courage. Before the case comes to trial, Greta expresses doubts and wants to move for a change of venue. Another crisis center worker responds, "We're going to see this thing through if it's the last thing we do." Yet at times Greta appears committed to the same goals and ideas as the feminists, hoping to help other women get out of their violent relationships.

The movie leaves open the question of what Greta truly felt and thought about her experiences. She seems to occupy the undecided middle ground between the ideals of the feminists and the pragmatic cynicism of a co-worker who asserts that men "all get rough once in a while . . . just like John," that it was "dumb" to leave a man, and that a few black eyes "come with the food on the table, the kid's shoes, the medical bills . . . it comes with the curse." This alternative view normalizes marital violence as a fact of everyday life (much as Burt had done in his defense strategy when he implied that making love was a normal way to resolve a violent episode). In addition, Greta's co-worker adds that the women at the crisis center are out of touch with the real world and that "if it was up to them this world wouldn't be anything but women." In asking Greta if she had "any idea what it's like out there with a kid and no man," the co-worker offers up a world view that accepts that most husbands are violent and that staying with a violent husband, rather than "just walking out," makes sense.

The film's resolution can be read as a vindication of the co-worker's view: in the television movie, feminist ideas for improving women's status are unable to offer Greta anything better than her marriage to John. The feminist view, although well articulated in the film, is proven to be ineffectual. This theme echoes the mainstream news coverage, which had recognized the need to protect wives from the possibility of marital rape while at the same time denying that this concept could have any practical application in the legal system. In both versions, it is possible to conclude that marital rape is a legitimate social problem for which no practical solution exists.

Although its portrayal of the Rideouts as a couple victimized by "the system" tends to trivialize Greta's experience, the television film does imply that Greta was raped, and that John was acquitted on the basis of a legal system controlled by men, a stacked jury, and an uncommitted district attorney. Additionally, questions about Gortmaker's political motivations and a critical focus on the way Burt twists the words of sympathetic witnesses combine to imply John's guilt without explicitly demonstrating or arguing for it. There remains in the film a good deal of ambiguity about John's guilt or innocence, although the trial has apparently not been conducted fairly. The difference in interpretation between the media reports and the film version is largely the result of the development of Greta's point of view in the film. By developing this perspective and focusing on Greta's experiences, the film adds legitimacy to her claim of rape.

The television film does not take a clear position on the specific case. The news coverage, in contrast, articulated neither of the Rideouts' positions fully but instead relied on a mythic framework to convey the validity of the traditional views of rape. In the television movie, then, the existence of two definitions of rape and consent is clearly established and both definitions are given legitimacy, yet no method for choosing between them is suggested. Although Greta's version of the rape incident is legitimized and given a tangible (visual) meaning, the causes and cures offered by feminists are not portrayed as effective or realistic. The representation of both feminists and defense attorneys as obstacles to be overcome by the two protagonists further undermines the otherwise well-articulated feminist perspective on rape and marital violence.

The fictional representation of the Rideout case developed the victim's perspective in a way not possible in news coverage by beginning the story before the start of the trial and including dramatic depictions of Greta hiding, running through the park, being dragged back to the apartment, and escaping to call the police—all from her own perspective. The film privileged the victim's position and problematized patriarchal marriage and the position of women within it, but ended with Greta and John reunited and looking hopefully toward the future.

Silent Witness

The first fictionalized text "based on" the Big Dan's case was the made-for-TV movie *Silent Witness*, which aired in October 1985. Like the Rideout TV movie, *Silent Witness* is sympathetic to the victim's perspective, and it presents a more complex version of the case than had appeared in news accounts. Unlike the Rideout film, it is only marginally related to the events of the real case. In *Silent Witness*, a lonely young woman goes to a bar looking for human contact. Three men talk and dance with her, buy her drinks, and then pull her to the ground; they carry her to a table and rape her almost directly in front of the bartender, the brother of one of the rapists, and the brother's wife. There are no cheering onlookers, as described in the Big Dan's case, and the victim commits suicide before the trial is completed.

Although the story is somewhat implausible, it serves to highlight (but does not directly articulate) significant elements of the reformed view of rape. The victim has difficulty obtaining justice even with the eventual help of the "silent witness" (the only female witness and the only one to come forward), and she cannot gain vindication without corroborating testimony. The rapists are depicted as "regular guys" who are friends, co-workers, and relatives of the film's protagonists. Although these men could be defined as "strangers" to the victim, they are not portrayed as marginal or unusual men. Finally, family ties in this movie are portrayed as significant factors in the possible achievement of justice, as the young protagonist couple resists testifying against their own relation. This text, however, completely erases all ethnic or racial themes from the original case and does not openly include any feminist characters or articulate feminist ideas.

A central theme of this film and of *The Accused* (the Hollywood version of the same case) is the notion, culled from mainstream news coverage, that victims of gang rape do not "deserve" what they get even if their social background, dress, habits and addictions, or sexual histories call into question their "victimhood" under the traditional model of rape. *Silent Witness* features a victim who is not only alcoholic but also prone to blackouts and accompanying memory lapses. Although the movie is unrealistic in depicting a district attorney who tries the case in spite of these facts, and in spite of the fact that there are no other witnesses to corroborate the victim's story, this narrative choice highlights the legal difficulties faced by a victim who presses for her right to be heard. In *Silent Witness* Patti, the victim, commits suicide after being viciously interrogated by the prosecuting attorney. She dies believing that there is no way she can win her case.

Although the victim plays a relatively minor role, the TV movie is nonetheless sympathetic to her position both in the scenes in which she appears and in the scenes after her death in which the film's protagonist, Anna (played by Valerie Bertinelli) testifies on her behalf. Patti appears only briefly after the rape scene: once during a visit from Anna and then during her testimony at trial. The final shot of Patti portrays her huddled in a corner contemplating suicide. These scenes are sympathetic to Patti, highlighting her personal struggles and her anguish at once again being a victim. (In this version, there is no doubt that the rape occurred, since the act is graphically and agonizingly depicted in the first ten minutes of the film: the three men are armed with a knife and a baseball bat they use to keep onlookers from stopping the rape; the victim's terrified screams are heard throughout the sequence.) When Anna visits Patti in her starkly furnished room, Patti almost immediately confesses her alcoholism and then admits to Anna that she cannot remember where the rape took place. As Anna confirms her suspicion that the rape occurred in the bar, Patti breaks down and Anna comforts her. Patti, visibly anguished, later says she is "just trying to live."

The key question in this movie is not whether the rape took place but whether Anna will testify against her brother-in-law John, who is one of the rapists. It seems clear throughout that Patti cannot obtain justice without Anna's testimony. The film's assumption that the uncorroborated word of the victim is insufficient to convict the gang rapists highlights an important element of rape law reform that was not at issue in the news coverage of the Big Dan's case. The bartender in the actual Big Dan's trial did testify to the rape, thus the issue of uncorroborated testimony was not within the realm of the news coverage. In *Silent Witness*, however, the bartender views the entire assault but testifies that he saw nothing, thereby leaving the rape reform issue of uncorroborated testimony as a relevant and central focus. As the victim testifies, she is verbally attacked by the prosecuting attorney, who forces her to read out loud from a newsletter article in which she confesses to "getting crazy" after a few drinks and sometimes having blackouts. She becomes more and more upset, eventually screaming at the attorney and collapsing on the stand. This is the last time Patti speaks in the film: she is later depicted huddled in a corner, and a report that she "tried" to make it but could not immediately follows.

It would be nearly impossible to avoid feeling compassion for Patti after watching this movie. She is portrayed as an extremely lonely young woman who can admit her problems but is unable to escape them—a person for whom nothing goes right. Although the defendants assert that she invited them to have sex, there can be little doubt after the rape scene that a violent crime has been committed. Anna and her husband, Kevin, sit in their car in shocked silence after witnessing the rape. Once inside the house, Anna becomes physically sick.

The rapists in *Silent Witness* are portrayed as rapists, not as "alleged" rapists or perpetrators of an "alleged incident" whose details are withheld from the viewer until the end of the film. They are also depicted as normal men with friends, families, and jobs. The primary perpetrator, Anna's brother-in-law, speaks very little during the film, and at the trial he simply denies that anything took place. He is depicted as fairly remorseless and able to continue on with his family relationships (with his wife, mother, and children) as if he were innocent. He and his friends, the other two rapists, are untroubled by their actions, and one tells Kevin that nothing happened, effectively challenging Kevin to define what he saw as a rape. By the end of the movie, Kevin says aloud that the woman was raped, thus admitting his brother's guilt.

The nearly complete silence of the rapists on the subject of their assault is significant: these men do not taunt the victim after the rape; they do not speak in objectifying terms about women in general or exhibit exaggerated "macho" behavior. They are portrayed as "average" men who perhaps suspect they may have done something wrong but do not really believe it. In depicting the rapists in this way, *Silent Witness* defines rapists according to the reformed view: they are not violent, angry stalkers or even unusually traditional, sexist, or macho men. In fact, their actions as a group do not seem especially wrong to them. And yet, no dialogue in the film asserts that rape is committed most often by seemingly normal men; the events and characters are left to the interpretation of viewers who may or may not have already heard about rape law reform.

Unlike the Rideout film, *Silent Witness* includes no characters who articulate feminist thoughts and understandings of rape or rape law reform. There are no feminist crisis workers or attorneys here (although there is one scene where a woman from the D.A.'s office tries to shame

Anna into testifying by telling her how the defense will be merciless to the victim). However, the TV movie does include some less directly expressed sympathies with the reform view. In addition to questioning the likelihood that a victim like Patti could obtain justice by simply telling the truth, the film highlights the connection between Patti and Anna, the only female witness. For various reasons none of the male witnesses will testify on Patti's behalf: the bartender is afraid of losing his business, Anna's husband refuses to hurt his brother, and two other men leave the bar at the beginning of the assault and claim to have seen nothing. Only Anna is shown having doubts: she repeatedly asks her husband what they should do about the situation, and he repeatedly tells her that they should just wait for the police to call on other witnesses to solve the crime. As it becomes increasingly evident that no other witnesses will come forward, Anna is more and more troubled by what she knows and continues to grapple with a course of action. After Patti's suicide she resolves to testify, against her husband's wishes, and goes so far as to move out of their home because the ordeal is ruining their relationship.

In a strange turn of events, Anna essentially stands in for the victim: She states that she represents all that is left of Patti. Anna becomes the subject of violent attacks from the prosecuting attorney and from her husband's family who, in their attempt to save John, his brother, have decided to spread lies about her motivations for testifying. Anna's infertility, her one-night stand with another witness to the crime, and her alleged vow of revenge for her husband's infidelity are all dragged into public view after her initial testimony. Although these plot turns are quite implausible, the movie nonetheless highlights real elements of a woman's experience during a rape trial: both the real victim and Anna are viciously attacked and made to look guilty, while in fact both have told the truth.

It would be possible to watch this film and fail to see the questions it raises about how victims obtain justice at trial: Patti could be read as a weak character, and Anna can be seen as a strong individual who triumphs because of her strength. A more likely reading might focus on the interpersonal constraints experienced by Anna (and later by Kevin) in attempting to follow her conscience despite constant pressure from Kevin's family to drop the case. This pressure is a focal point several times during the film. In one scene Anna returns home to a surprise birthday party in her honor. Friends and members of Kevin's family present her with a check for $3000 toward her "dream home." Immediately recognizing this as hush money, Anna asserts that she will never forget what she saw and leaves the party. In the scene that follows, Kevin and John's mother invites Anna for a walk and argues that even if the rape happened and the victim's life is ruined, it would make no sense to ruin other lives as well by testifying against "the boys." In other scenes Anna comforts her sister-in-law, who is also her best friend, assuring her that her husband will be released, and even lying to protect her from the truth about his violence against Patti. Anna is clearly trapped in a web of family and friendships; she literally has to break off these connections in order to act according to her conscience.

Thus, while this film highlights important issues related to rape and rape reform, it may be seen as placing them in a secondary position to other themes. There is no clear or direct articulation of feminist themes, but a woman is shown working through a dilemma and coming to a somewhat feminist conclusion: obtaining justice for the "silenced" victim and clearing her own name are the right courses to pursue and, as such, are preferable to continuing to be tied to family members who collude to protect one of their own from punishment. It may be possible to view this film without identifying any of its elements as "feminist," but the film may also be read as legitimizing feminist views as simply the right way to believe and act, regardless of ideology.

Silent Witness ends with Kevin's decision to corroborate Anna's version of what they both witnessed, and the movie concludes much like the Rideout film, with the husband and wife reunited and apparently ready to face the future together. Rapping's analysis of *Silent Witness* argues that this is an implausible ending for a woman who has been through such a transformative experience. She cites the working-class identities of Anna and her husband the "garbage man," noting that "for working class heroines—those few that TV allows—it is an either/or situation. Keep the man or continue to grow and change" (Rapping 1992, 77). Rape law reform in *Silent Witness* certainly does not provide any alternatives for Anna or Patti. Like the character of Greta in *Rape and Marriage*, Anna returns to her husband. However, unlike John Rideout, Anna's husband is caring and nonviolent. He is able to accept her strength and is willing to defy (and even be rejected by) his family in order to stay with her. And yet, significantly, neither film portrays feminism as a useful force for helping working-class women deal with the issues and problems that confront them.

The two made-for-television movies *Rape and Marriage: The Rideout Case* and *Silent Witness* both privilege the victim's point of view. This is perhaps not surprising, given Rapping's observation that a significant proportion of made-for-TV movies comprise a "women's genre," with women as the intended audience, interpersonal relationships as the central subject matter, and women cast as the protagonists who must work within the constraints placed on them by a patriarchal social structure. Hollywood films, in contrast, are less likely to present a woman's point of view and are much less likely to address a primarily female audience. Rapping attributes this to the supposition that men purchase most tickets to theatrical films while women are more likely to make their own viewing choices at home (Rapping 1992, 82). Whatever the reason, made-for-TV movies have a far better chance of presenting a story from a female perspective than do Hollywood films. Hollywood almost always assumes the male perspective, asking viewers to identify and sympathize primarily with male protagonists. The Hollywood version of the Big Dan's case, however, is in many ways an anomaly: it takes on a female perspective and openly articulates feminist ideas regarding rape.

The Hollywood Version of the Big Dan's Case

In *All That Hollywood Allows*, Jackie Byars discusses the importance of ideological struggle within film texts in much the same terms as Rapping's discussion of the made-for-TV movie. Byars notes:

We are never outside of ideology, and the patriarchal center to a great extent, though not completely, constructs its margins, but the occupants of the margins can resist. We are never able to completely "step outside" patriarchal discourse. . . . Patriarchy is not monolithic, but its dominance influences even the feminist discourses that challenge it. . . . Ideological struggle is everywhere evident, and patriarchy only partially constructs its opposition. Not even cinematic language is without feminine influences. (Byars 1990, 33)

Film texts, as products of popular culture, will show evidence of ideological struggle between dominant patriarchal ideology and feminist resistance, although theatrical films are likely to be less thorough in their articulation of feminist ideas and less directly designed for female audiences than are made-for-TV movies.

In addition, as Rapping notes, made-for-TV movies are more simplistic in their delivery of a social message and are more likely to focus on family themes (Rapping 1992). Theatrical films, which make money through box office sales rather than through product advertising, are often less directly tied to family and social improvement, and can be more open to a range of interpretations.

In 1988, the Hollywood film *The Accused*, loosely based on the events of the Big Dan's case, was released, starring Jodie Foster and Kelly McGillis. The film disavowed any connection with the Big Dan's case, but the similarities between the movie and the actual facts of the Big Dan's case are many: in the film, a single woman enters a bar and has a drink with a waitress, the only other woman in the bar. After flirting and dancing with a group of men, she is violently raped on a pinball machine by three of them, while three others cheer them on. Several onlookers watch without intervening. Half naked, the woman runs out into the street and is picked up by a passing truck and taken to the hospital.

There are, however, several significant differences between the case and the Hollywood film. In the film, the three rapists plea-bargain and never go to trial; the three cheering onlookers are prosecuted and convicted. Sarah Tobias, the victim in the film (played by Jodie Foster), has no children, and the issues of psychiatric care, previous claims of rape, and welfare are not included in the story (the victim's character is brought into question according to traditional beliefs about rape in other ways: she is depicted as uneducated, sexually active, provocatively dressed on the night of the rape, and fond of drugs, alcohol, and vulgar language). Just as the television version of the Rideout case had stripped down the relevant issues to questions about forcible compulsion and the legitimacy of the crime of marital rape, *The Accused* strips away most of the complex legal issues and the political context that were part of the Big Dan's case: the wisdom of using cameras in the courtroom, the significance of the defendants' ethnic identity, and the heated cultural climate in which the original trial took place.

As in *Silent Witness* what is left are key remaining questions from the news coverage: whether or not a woman could "ask for" or provoke a violent gang rape and whether or not justice, and a right to speak, could be achieved through the heroic efforts of the victim. *The Accused* focuses more clearly on the theme of victim justice through attaining voice and ends much more optimistically. Yet the film's ending—successful convictions *and* a triumphant victim—sidesteps difficult questions about how victims judge the costs and benefits of testifying. Meanwhile, the Hollywood version exhibits many of the same characteristics as the fictionalized account of the Rideout case. It presents a highly personalized account largely from the perspective of the victim, clearly articulating feminist ideas about rape while simultaneously raising issues of class status and justice.

In the film, the victim works untiringly to convince district attorney Katheryn Murphy (played by Kelly McGillis) to prosecute the case so that she can have a chance to tell her version of the rape to the world. From an early scene where the district attorney plea-bargains the freedom of the three rapists, the victim does not waver from her goal of achieving justice and voice; by the end of the film she has achieved both. As in the news discourse, the victim's valiant efforts to clear her name and obtain justice are central themes. Sarah Tobias is motivated primarily by the desire to have her name formally and legally cleared so that no one will think she is pitiable or shameful because she was raped; neither was she guilty of provoking the attack or deserving of such violence.

After the initial plea bargain, Tobias expresses her feelings and reasons for wanting to be heard: "He figures I'm just a piece of shit. Everybody figures I'm a piece of shit. Why not? You told 'em that. I never got to tell nobody nothin'. You did all my talkin' for me."[3] In showing Sarah dancing, talking, and drinking prior to the rape, the film highlights circumstances that have traditionally been used to discredit rape claimants. The placement of the rape at the end of the film allows viewers ample time to formulate their own ideas about innocence and guilt based on their own attitudes about rape myths. The graphic and prolonged depiction of the rape could certainly have shocked some viewers into rethinking their ideas about rape victims and "victim precipitation."

Film reviews picked up on this theme, noting that Tobias defies the definitions and abuses heaped on her throughout the film and refuses to change or make excuses for her sexual behavior (Johnson 1988, 61). The best example of Tobias's refusal to apologize or accept any responsibility for provoking her own rape is near the end of the film, where she admits having said, "I'd like to take that guy home and fuck his brains out right in front of Larry." She adds, "So what? It was just a joke." Tobias seems to be unable to comprehend how this information could be relevant to the case: It is impossible for her to understand how anyone could think she asked for or deserved what had happened to her, even though she has a prior police record, uses drugs and alcohol frequently, and lives with a boyfriend described by another character as a "dealer." Tobias expresses a feminist perspective on rape, speaking at length about the degradation and humiliation she has experienced, and insists that the men responsible be brought to justice. She insists that her horrifying experience should be publicly and legally validated as such.

As Byars notes, "even as feminists have developed the techniques involved in 'reading against the grain' of mainstream texts, they have ignored both the systematically resistant discourses within the texts and the pleasures to be found in resistance" (Byars 1991, 34). Clear echoes of feminist discourse about rape are evident in *The Accused*, although only narrow and specific elements of this discourse survive in the film. *The Accused* produces a narrative in which both central characters, the victim and the district attorney (Tobias convinces the D.A. to help her fight for her rights) achieve their goals. The D.A. wins a tough case, while the victim wins back her personal pride and integrity. To successfully complete the narrative, the film rewrites the verdict: In the real trial those who had not touched the woman were not convicted. The film verdict extends the triumph of the female D.A. and the victim by suggesting the guilt of all those present in the bar, echoing the real-life victim's assertion that all who watched were also guilty. The film expands on the mainstream news themes of the victim's heroic search for justice and the idea that women do not provoke or ask for violent gang rape.

It would be possible to read the film's heavy emphasis on the traditional elements of rape conceptualization—non-credibility of the victim depicted through drug and alcohol use, clothing choices, interpersonal behavior, social class, and a sexually active lifestyle—in a different way. For example, they could be read as depicting a victim whose behavior contributed to or provoked her own rape. Byars contends both that "textual analysis must attempt to account for the way cultural texts make available the diversity of interpretations we know to be available," and that at the same time "it must attend to the privileging of certain interpretations over others" (Byars 1991, 36). Although multiple readings of these factors are certainly possible, the privileged reading holds that the personal experiences and feelings of Tobias, the protagonist, are important, and their validation requires that the men responsible for her suffering be punished. Just as some news stories took the side of the victim in this case, several elements of the film combine to suggest that many behaviors traditionally considered inappropriately seductive for women—including wearing revealing clothing and dancing suggestively—do not add up to asking for or deserving rape. In the motivations and actions of the protagonist, the film portrays as heroic the common woman struggling against the legal system and cultural bias.

In one scene, Tobias barges into the district attorney's home during a dinner party after Katheryn Murphy has just allowed the three rapists to go free by plea-bargaining for a reduced charge of reckless endangerment. Tobias's trampy appearance, language, and ferocious demeanor provide a stark contrast to the guests' evening attire and the expensive decor of the attorney's apartment. Furious, Tobias unleashes a string of foul language that highlights the contrast between the upper-middle-class dinner guests and the outraged rape victim. The scene, emphasizing the ways in which Tobias lacks legal credibility, also reveals her resolve and personal integrity. It is a turning point in the film that signals to both Murphy and the viewing audience that Tobias is not a helpless "victim" and that she is not going to drop the case.

In some ways the film directly critiques the traditional view of rape. Sarah Tobias is continually having to learn to "think legal" to comprehend why certain aspects of her life are relevant to the question of whether she was raped. Early in the film the district attorney asks her extremely personal questions. When Sarah demands, "What the fuck kinda question is that?" the D.A. responds:

it's a question you're gonna be asked on the stand. You're also gonna be asked if Larry or any other man has ever hit you and if you liked it. You're gonna be asked about your drug bust and how many drinks a day you have to smooth out the edges. And how many joints. And how often you go to bars alone and whether or not you wear underwear when you go to them and which diseases you've caught and how many abortions you've had. . . . It's the defense's job to show the jury that you're a rotten witness because you've got a rotten character.

Tobias responds, "I got a rotten character? You ain't gonna defend me because I'm some low-class bimbo, right?" The emphasis on Tobias's "low-class," sexually active, drug-using character, as well as sympathetic scenes that portray the effects of the rape on her personal life, suggest that no one asks for gang rape, that gang rape is not an unconscious desire, and that it is not the deserved outcome of any woman's behavior.

Since Tobias has much to hide from public view, including the fact that she smokes marijuana and enjoys a few drinks "to smooth out the edges," she fails to mention a few details to the district attorney. Most significantly, she neglects to mention that while she was in the bar, before the rape, she commented to her waitress friend that she would like to screw one of the men to get back at her boyfriend. This omission leads to arguments between the two about the nature of rape trials and to a monologue from the D.A. warning Tobias that she will be on trial as much as the defendants. At issue are misconceptions about the nature of rape, consent, a victim's character, and female sexuality. Tobias might not receive a "fair trial" because the defense would assert that she "asked for it."

Although the film is fairly open in its critique of traditional views, it is also overly optimistic in its guilty verdict for the three men who only looked on and cheered. Indeed, *The Accused* portrays the legal process as a vehicle for the vindication of female victims. This portrayal is directly contradicted by the real experiences of rape victims, especially those who, like Sarah Tobias, have "questionable" backgrounds. While manifestly articulating a feminist perspective on rape, *The Accused* also misrepresents the reality of rape and rape trials as understood and critiqued by feminist rape law reformers.

In addition, by purging the film of racial or ethnic tensions, and by portraying the story as a personal quest for justice for the district attorney and victim, the filmmakers avoided a difficult yet important question under discussion during the actual trial: Would the Big Dan's defendants have been treated differently in both the news coverage and the trial itself had they not been members of an ethnic minority who did not speak English? Certainly the film is not to be condemned because it does not include minority rapists. Yet, there are more than just two possibilities for the representation of these men, and not all would need to elide or reinforce the traditional racist ideology of rape. For example, by depicting a mixed-race group of rapists and a black man as the one who repents and testifies, the film could have given this complex topic the attention it deserves. What is significant is that both *Silent Witness* and *The Accused* completely eliminate the issue of race and ethnicity.

The Hollywood version places responsibility for the rape on an individualized "macho" attitude, similar to the news media's incrimination of an individual ethnic community. In the Hollywood version of the case, defendants are one-dimensional and unsympathetic. Although the film includes a fraternity member among the rapists, more detailed character development is reserved for the defendant who is depicted as the most instrumental in goading the rapists into action (only this defendant appears in scenes other than the rape, arrest, and trial scenes). This character, who wears a scorpion tattoo on his arm and is heard arguing with his female companion and police, is portrayed as being practically incapable of seeing women as human beings. In one scene he states, "No, I don't know her. She's a whore. The last time I saw her she was doing a sex show . . . next time she does another show tell her I'll be right there to cheer her on."

This defendant is a large man with dark hair and eyes. In a key scene, he spots Tobias in a record store and approaches her with the one-liner, "Haven't I seen you somewhere before?" When she drops her keys, he stoops to pick them up and remembers her "Sexy Sadie" license plates from the night at the bar. Immediately he begins taunting her, imitating intercourse with his fingers. Laughing maniacally, he says, "Do I know you! Sexy Sadie. Oh, do I remember YOU!" This characterization of the primary defendant reinforces the traditional explanation of stranger rape as a crime committed by easily identifiable, sexually aggressive men. As in the Big Dan's news coverage, where this problem was framed in the context of the Portuguese community and not treated as a larger social phenomenon, the problem here is displaced onto a particularly "male chauvinist" individual whose exaggerated sexist attitudes fuel the rape. The film does not explain or offer insight into where such attitudes come from or how general social practices encourage or even develop them. It does not question the traditional myths about rapists with regard to race and ethnicity, nor does it articulate the rape law reform alternatives for any of these components of traditional understandings.

By largely limiting the characterization to this hyper-masculine and obnoxious man, and by clearly associating sexist ideas and words with him, the filmmakers emphasize the injustice of placing a victim on trial in all cases of rape. The victim is portrayed as much more human and sympathetic than this defendant, while the other defendants are portrayed as easily recognizable types, such as the smug and arrogant fraternity boy and the insecure follower easily swayed by peer pressure.

By openly underscoring the victim's need for eye-witness testimony, the film argues that the word of a victim still is not sufficient to obtain a conviction, even in these extreme circumstances. Additionally, the emphasis on the victim's personal determination and the film's positive ending (the trial results in convictions) tend to suggest, as did some news stories, that the responsibility for rape convictions rests on victims, who should report and prosecute the crime and be willing to undergo a stressful and potentially humiliating trial experience. In the Hollywood version, Sarah Tobias even confronts the key eye-witness and asks him why he is "doing this" to her when he threatens to withdraw his cooperation with the prosecution. This idea of personal achievement through hard work emphasizes the great lengths to which one must go to achieve justice as a victim, but it also masks the reality of many victims who find that their cases are not strong enough, despite their efforts.

The themes in *The Accused*—the rape victim's struggle for vindication, the importance of coming forward and persevering—were given wide circulation when actress Kelly McGillis told her "story" of having been raped. *People* magazine reported that she agreed to publish her story to help other rape victims and to raise awareness of the fact that a woman is sexually assaulted every six minutes (McGillis 1988, 155). This statistic also was included in an epilogue to the film, along with the information that one in four victims is attacked by more than one assailant. McGillis suggested that progress had been made in the way rape victims see their experience: She remembered that she had at first believed that the rape was her own fault (158). Eventually, she had come to understand that the rape was not her fault, and through much effort she was able to regain some self-esteem. After a lengthy description of the effects of the attack on her psychological and physical well-being, McGillis concluded that victims remain victims as long as they do not prosecute their attackers and that talking about the assault is the only method for preventing rape in the future (160). In effect, McGillis translated a central theme of the film through an explanation of her own experience and feelings about rape. It is a theme culled from mainstream media attitudes toward rape, which reflects the major points of consensus on the issues of rape law reform: Brutal rapes have nothing to do with consent. Women who fight back should be seen as heroines in their own lives.

The Accused represents a modality of news coverage by honing in on certain elements from mainstream news reports and suggesting some of the same conclusions: There was some sentiment during the Big Dan's proceedings that the victim was heroic in pursuing the charges and going through with the two trials, and there were expressions of outrage against those who thought she had asked to be gang raped. Those who thought she deserved it were treated unsympathetically in both the news and fictional versions. In a sense, however, the film was a better vehicle for providing a clear "discussion" of the two sides of the issue.

In the film, Sarah Tobias is vilified by the traditional rules, yet the outcome reinforces the idea that such a victim is deserving of justice and could not have asked to be raped. In *The Accused*, the trial serves as the place where Tobias finally gets to tell her version of what happened, and it is during her testimony that the film finally depicts the rape, as if to contend that the reality of it did not exist outside of her telling of it.

*   *   *

One of the primary goals of rape law reform, and of the larger feminist movements that have been active in the last two centuries, has been to ensure just treatment for women, who, as human beings with valid experiences, deserve to have representation in public discourses in the legal arena, in books, in news coverage, and in everyday conversation. Thus the significance of the victim's perspective that is emphasized in *Rape and Marriage*, *Silent Witness*, and *The Accused* should not be underestimated. The fictionalized accounts of the Rideout and Big Dan's cases were better able than mainstream news to articulate coherent and logical feminist views of rape law reform. However, in each case the film's central narrative works to mask and contradict the feminist message within it. And while the narrative structure of *The Accused* allows for the detailed articulation of elements of the feminist ideology about rape — ideas which had also been legitimized by mainstream news coverage — the film's focus on the personal heroism and strength of Sarah Tobias also serves to limit and contain the further expression of feminist ideas about rape and rape law reform. The choice not to treat issues of racism and ethnic bias in both *Silent Witness* and *The Accused* is also significant: if it is possible that "justice" for the victim was served in the Big Dan's case because the defendants were marginalized by national origin and language, then this issue should receive an open examination. So far, the issue remains unexplored.

Forgive Me

Intended as an explanation of her motives during the events that took place from 1977 to 1985, Cathleen Webb's confessional narrative *Forgive Me*, coauthored with Marie Chapian (coauthor of several books on Christian themes), was released in 1987. The autobiographical account centers on the emotional deprivation of Webb's childhood, offering it as an explanation for the lie she allegedly invented about her rape by Gary Dotson. The book received poor reviews and was out of print within two years; the television movie that was reportedly proposed during the height of the publicity surrounding the case was never realized. As a story written *by* the "victim," *Forgive Me* differs greatly from *Rape and Marriage: The Rideout Case, Silent Witness,* and *The Accused* both in content and purpose.[4] The book fits solidly within the tradition of the confessional autobiographical novel. Such novels, as Doody notes, are "an apology for the self, a realization of the self in social or ethical terms" (Doody 1980, 20). Webb's alleged purpose in writing the book was to explain her actions through a careful description of how she had become such an effective liar, and to offer an apology for having harmed Dotson. In Doody's terms, authors of such novels "in their full-scale explanations of themselves . . . also talk about their nature, their identity. However real their crimes may be, their outlawry is also a symbolic state or metaphor for their estrangement from a community" (20). The purpose of Webb's book, then, was to ask forgiveness and thus plead for acceptance back into the larger ethical community of Christians.

Forgive Me, like the news coverage of the case, serves as a reinforcement of traditional rape myths. Webb makes use of feminist and dominant discourses concerning rape to position herself within a traditional ethical community where women are not ambitious or overtly sexual and where alleged rape victims could easily fool well-meaning jurors and judges. In her search for what Doody calls "therapeutic purgation" (18), Webb selected traditional discourses about rape and gender as part of her newfound discursive and ethical community. In Doody's terms, Webb turned to an audience that would validate her, "toward a community . . . not merely an aesthetic relationship but a moral order as well" (37). In doing so, she positioned herself against feminist discourse about rape.

Along with news coverage of Webb's recantation, *Forgive Me* took part in a backlash "reexamination" of rape reform without ever explicitly articulating the reform position. The characters that emerge are Webb and the members of her family. As the book progresses, tension and conflict develop between Webb and her elderly aunt. The tensions that result in her allegedly false accusation of Dotson are resolved through her conversion to Christianity, which leads in turn to her public recantation. Thus, the story is organized as a religious journey that ends successfully in her acceptance of God and redemption from sin:

I explained how I had gone to church and had always wanted to be good so I could get to heaven. But I knew I had done bad things. . . . I never felt I was good enough for His acceptance. . . . I began naming sins I had committed. "Forgive Me," I prayed. "That sin put You on the cross. Thank You for forgiving me." . . . I knew I was now close to God and accepted by Him. . . . Then as suddenly as a blast from a rifle, and as ferocious, I saw a man. His shoulders were shaking; he was sobbing before a judge. *Oh God, no, not that, please! Not that!* (Webb and Chapian 1987, 161–162; emphasis in original)

Webb describes herself as an abandoned child who had been shuffled from home to home. The book represents a modality of news content in that it echoes the same messages Webb had emphasized during the hearings, with added explanations of her motivations. She focuses on her lies, not only about Dotson, but also about a number of things she felt had to be kept hidden from the adults around her. Written half in first person (in Webb's voice) and half in third person (in Chapian's voice), the book offers a detailed account of how and why Webb had learned to lie so proficiently.

Focusing on her conversion to Christianity after her marriage and on her devotion to family and church, Webb asserts that during her adolescent years she had big plans for herself. This ambitious future is described as part of her earlier sinful existence, whereas the Webb at the end of the book has "throw[n] off [her] blue jeans in favor of dresses and skirts," observing that "it used to be that I wanted to take the world by storm; to be a successful executive. . . . [now] I was even starting to enjoy homemaking. . . . Who would have guessed I could change so much?" (172). The ethical lines are clearly drawn with the older Webb, in opposition to her younger self, cast solidly within a traditional discourse of femininity.

Webb clearly condemns her former self while emphasizing the peacefulness and happiness of her new lifestyle, which includes baking, using a wood stove, and patronizing neighborhood farmers (172). Insofar as *Forgive Me* functions to describe the motives for Webb's actions, it presents these actions as the result of an unhappy childhood and of a sinful, "unsaved" nature. The book works within the traditional understanding of rape by emphasizing the fabricated claim of rape and the sinful and scheming nature of a "promiscuous" young girl who had easily fooled attorneys, her foster parents, a judge, and a jury into thinking she had been brutally raped.

Webb's account of the events in her life that led up to the events in the Dotson case emphasize her lying more than any other aspect of her life. Webb asserts that she had developed great skill at lying because of her overly protective guardian, who refused to let her so much as go outside without an excuse. *Forgive Me* details many of the lies Webb told during her life with "Aunt Nellie" and highlights her expertise in lying convincingly.

Toward the end of the book, where the events of 1977–1985 are described, the emphasis is still on lying. In Chapian's voice, the book describes how Webb had effectively staged a dramatic performance designed to convince her foster-parents and the police that she had been raped. However, Chapian argues, once Webb started lying she was trapped in subsequent lies that eventually became public against her wishes and expectations (139). In addition, *Forgive Me* draws direct connections between the romance fiction Cathy had been reading and the story she fabricated. Again in Chapian's voice, the book asserts that Cathy had been fond of romance novels and had read one featuring three drunken men who violently rape a woman. Chapian asserts that although such novels do not cause false rape accusations, she believes that "for someone who was confused, and emotionally distraught, these books provided the script for the lie she had decided to tell" (139). Although *Forgive Me* notes that Webb was naive in staging her own rape because she did not realize that "a violent rapist does more than leave little pin scratches and fingernail marks on his victims" (138), it nonetheless asserts that it was easy for everyone else to believe the story because they wanted to. By describing the words written on Webb's stomach as "pin scratches," the book downplays the corroborative evidence that had helped to convict Gary Dotson and implies instead that the system is stacked from the start *in favor of* the alleged victim.

Forgive Me thus contends that everyone believed Webb's story because of their traditional beliefs about rapists and victims: they were willing to go along with Webb during the original trial when she seemed to fit the classic portrait of an innocent rape victim. However, instead of arguing in favor of rape reform views and against harmful traditional ideas, Webb used these same rape myths during her recantation, in which she utilized the preexisting beliefs that rape victims lie and that rapists have a certain kind of character that Dotson did not possess. In her recantation testimony she emphasized how easy it had been to falsify the rape. In the book, she asserts that people are wrong to hold traditional beliefs about rape at the same time that she situates her story within these very myths to obtain credence. By redrawing her 1979 character (which at trial had been that of a sixteen-year-old virgin) as one of a manipulative and skillful liar, she simply shifts herself from the realm of the acceptable victim to that of the unacceptable victim. However, both characterizations fit into the traditional framework for understanding rape. Webb and Chapian depict a young girl who lied about rape out of fear of repercussions in case of pregnancy—the same strategy outlined in legal writings to justify the hostile treatment of victims at trial.

Chapian's description of Webb's reasons for lying also fit into the traditional expressions of legal apprehensions regarding the testimony of rape victims. Chapian argues that old-fashioned attitudes about sex had led Webb to misunderstand sexuality and to greatly fear the repercussions of her sexual activity. Chapian notes that Webb was taught that "sex was bad," that the outside world was a dangerous place, and that "Cathy was fragile, incapable of handling danger, and vulnerable to evil ways . . . the emphasis was on shame" (76). By this logic, then, Webb learned that the only forgivable sexual contact was forced and nonconsensual: when she feared pregnancy, she claimed rape.

The book also relies on readers' doubts about the veracity of rape victims and the inability of the jury system to distinguish between truthful and untruthful victims. Echoing Matthew Hale's warning about the emotional nature of the crime of rape and the compelling nature of the wronged victim as witness, Webb remembered the reaction of her foster parents, Carol and Bernie Smith, on their arrival at the police station on the night of the rape: Carol and Officer Anna Carroll were both visibly upset, and Carol asked Webb if she had been raped. At that point, Webb explains, she felt caught: "What could I do? *They already believed. I pressed my head against her and nodded yes. When I did I felt . . . as though there were no going back" (106; emphasis in original).

Webb's story includes several hints as to why rape has traditionally been considered an especially heinous crime. Her foster father was personally hurt by news of the alleged crime, and all the adults in the situation were shocked and determined to "get the guy" because of what he had done to her. Her story, though false, was accepted by police, parents, and others because it played into their fears and emotional responses to the horrible nature of rape. Her explanation follows the corresponding logic that such fears and the tensions in relationships to parents and other authority figures provide motivations for women to lie about rape and follow through with their claims.

Webb also outlines the parameters required to convict a rapist under a traditional view of rape. She and coauthor Chapian describe the disjuncture between the characterizations of herself and Dotson at the 1979 trial and in 1985, noting specifically that Webb appeared to be a "pure" and legitimate rape victim since she had good grades and was mistakenly described as a young virgin. Chapian notes that Dotson, on the other hand, had a criminal record and was a high school dropout. The prosecution was able to obtain a conviction in part because, as Chapian quotes another observer, she looked "like apple pie, like the figure on top of a wedding cake" (136).

Webb's description of Dotson's character also added credence to the media's suggestion that there was something a little mysterious about a legal system that would convict him based on her testimony. For the most part, *Forgive Me* proclaims Dotson's innocence while failing to find any validity in the legal logic that had sent him to prison, noting only at one point that Judge Richard Samuels, who had ruled on the recanted testimony, had said that the law took a "jaundiced view" of recantations generally (199). *Forgive Me* also echoes the news coverage sentiment about Dotson's mother: Webb describes her as gracious in her attitude throughout the trial. Webb frequently reiterates her thoughts about the

Dotson family and what she had done to them. She cites the connection between her feelings for her own children and Mrs. Dotson's feelings for Gary as a strong motivation for coming forward.

Given Webb's avowed purpose in writing the book, there is little chance that *Forgive Me* could have included expressions of rape law reform ideas. Instead, the book offers an example of how a text can perpetuate traditional ideas about rape while appearing to critique them. The book also extends traditional fears about the ease of false accusation. *Forgive Me* undertakes a thoroughly personal explanation of the motives of Cathleen Crowell Webb, focusing on her childhood of neglect and abandonment as an explanation for her proficiency in lying. However, this proficiency is also rooted in ideas about femininity, the female body, and sex, which, while presented as highly personal, are likely to be shared by many. Webb and Chapian's discussion of adolescent shame and fear about sex echoes sentiments that are widespread. To the extent that her feelings ring true, Webb's explanations for her actions can be generalized to other young women who might be "caught" in similar situations. In this way, the book suggests that rape is easily falsifiable and that rape should continue to be treated as a special crime with relation to corroborating evidence at trial. But the book ignores unresolved questions about corroborating evidence that had existed at the 1979 trial: a large semen stain that could not reasonably have been caused by intercourse with her boyfriend several days before the alleged rape, and the letters on her stomach, which, if self-inflicted, would have been written upside-down and backward.

Conclusion

The post-trial accounts of the Rideout, Big Dan's, and Dotson cases all represented modalities of news coverage that were highly personalized, and all presented the victim's point of view. In the first three mass-mediated texts, the fictional mode enabled the elimination and distillation of key issues for consideration. In this way, the emergence of the fictionalized texts based on these highly publicized rape cases can be seen as the second phase in a complex process through which dominant ideology adjusts and accepts part of an oppositional ideology, even as it sets limits on such change. These accommodations take place discursively, in that they are adjudicated in mainstream, public communication. The fictionalized texts based on these cases picked up on and more clearly articulated the limits set by mainstream news, delving deeper into more personalized issues and dramatizing some of the difficult choices involved. The fictionalized texts based on *Rideout* and *Big Dan's* were more amenable to the expression of feminist views and to the portrayal of a victim's perspective, thereby further legitimizing the changes accepted in news discourse and offering a coherent oppositional view; however, these fictionalized texts eliminated references to more complex issues and stopped short of full-fledged critiques of the status quo.

The Rideout television film emphasized the nature of violent marital relationships, clearly privileging the victim's perspective throughout the story. The film's structure as a romance, however, blurred the focus of Greta's perspective by suggesting that the Rideouts were equally victimized by the legal process: both were swept up by larger forces while still longing for each other. While the violence in marriage was articulated from a feminist point of view (including discussion of the economic entrapment of women), feminists were portrayed as self-centered and pushy, and as equally ruthless as the defense attorneys. The romance format included a parallel structure that balanced shots of Greta and crisis center workers with shots of John and defense attorneys, such that feminists and defense attorneys constituted the outside world against which the couple struggled to reunite. In effect, while Greta's real experience of rape was legitimized, the corresponding emphasis on the victimization of both Rideouts, on the basis of their class, undermined a clearly feminist reading of the film and even suggested, as had the news coverage, that the feminist view was theoretically viable but not practically useful.

Silent Witness championed female perspectives of solidarity by literally substituting the witness Anna for the rape victim on the witness stand. This version portrayed the rapists as young white men who were normal by most standards and were loved and even protected by their families, showing, in effect, that rapists are not necessarily crazy or otherwise marginalized strangers. Finally, *Silent Witness* presented a very flawed victim who nonetheless appeared to deserve both compassion and justice.

In *The Accused* the victim's perspective was even more clearly privileged: her character was thoroughly developed while none of the defendants were depicted as remotely sympathetic. Like *Rape and Marriage*, this film rejected issues that had been important in the original case, focusing instead on a particular issue. The film exaggerated the traditional definition of a "bad character" in Sarah Tobias while at the same time depicting her as the victim of a violent gang rape. Since *The Accused* followed Tobias's struggle to tell her own story, and to find justice, its structure was stacked in her favor. However, the narrative of the quest also served to elide and overly personalize salient cultural issues as well as legal considerations. In particular, the cause of the rape was suggested to be the extremely macho attitude of the men in the bar, and of one man in particular. The film's successful conclusion, which involved convictions for the onlookers, suggested in turn that hard work and determination result in justice — although the history of rape law reform belies such a conclusion.

Analysis of these three texts reveals that fiction offers the important element of point of view, which can go far in enabling the expression of feminist rape law reform ideas in the public sphere. Nevertheless, the narratives covered up or distorted contradictions and problems that exist in the general culture and that were manifested in these particular cases. Excessive personalization in fiction, as in news, effectively restricts any larger discussion of social problems while sometimes even suggesting that they have been resolved.

The fictional treatments of the Rideout and Big Dan's cases allowed a more fully articulated critique of patriarchy and its laws but without offering solutions outside of those power structures. One offered a romantic ending as the resolution to ongoing marital violence; the second also concluded with the protagonist couple reunited; and the third offered only the perseverance of victims as a means for gaining greater justice in rape cases. In these ways, these fictional versions resembled other ostensibly "feminine" fictional forms. They provided information about problems that confront contemporary women from the perspective of those women but did not offer radical alternatives to the institutions they exposed.

Cathleen Crowell Webb's book *Forgive Me* is also highly personalized in its explanation of why Gary Dotson was wrongly sent to prison. The book offers an example of how traditional ideas about rape can be reinforced even as they appear to be criticized. In this it shares with the three films a use of narrative construction that distorts and resists alternative definitions of rape by suppressing conflicting information that would provide alternate readings of the texts. As an expression of backlash against rape law reform, *Forgive Me* also differs from the other three texts: Webb relies on traditional myths for the plausibility of her story.

Notes

1. All quotes are taken directly from the TV movie, which is available for rental at video stores.

2. In Helen Benedict's book *Virgin or Vamp: How the Press Covers Sex Crimes* (New York: Oxford, 1992), Greta Rideout protests this portrayal as inaccurate, asserting that she was not promiscuous or prone to fantasies.

3. All direct quotes in this section are taken from the film.

4. It could be argued that *Forgive Me* is completely different from the other texts examined here in that it is nonfiction; however, confessional novels are to some extent fictionalized in their selective presentation of facts and events, and Webb's book is no exception.

Chapter 6
Conclusion

This book began with the observation that many writers and thinkers have recently paused to consider the surprising resistance to change encountered by modern feminist movements, including the movement for rape law reform. The key question has become: Is pessimism warranted, or should the success of contemporary social movements be measured by some standard other than their originally stated goals? Although the rape reform project has not been wholly embraced by mainstream culture, significant changes in national level discourses may yet constitute very real success. The terms of the mainstream understanding of rape are still being negotiated in relation to the feminist reformulation. The sheer number of rape cases that are now receiving national attention and the magnitude of the attention they receive are significant signs that the subject of rape is currently important to U.S. culture. The resulting discourses have enacted a visible power struggle over meanings and truths. This book has examined some of these power struggles by interrogating the content and frameworks of the mythic narratives surrounding highly publicized rape trials. For those interested in the progress of rape reform, this exploration has yielded cause for hope in some areas and discouragement in others.

It is discouraging to find that even after centuries of women's struggle to gain a voice in the public spheres of politics and culture, and after decades of working to articulate victims' experiences of rape trials, news stories still do not include coherent or complete depictions of these experiences. The requirements of news discourse, combined with a focus on trial coverage as an arena for discussing rape, have worked to limit and fragment the expression of feminist ideas about rape in the public realm. News accounts of trials are not well suited for discussion of social movement issues, yet most mainstream news coverage of these agendas is tied to specific trials. The concurrent emphases on dramatic conflict, personalization of issues, and legitimization through the citing of expert sources, combined with a tendency to avoid in-depth discussions of logic or contextualizing elements, help to contain or distort rape law reform meanings in mainstream news coverage. The result is coverage that fits the mythic framework in which the traditional understanding of rape is implied even when the content is not explicitly antagonistic to reform.

Examination of public discourses surrounding three high-profile rape trials has provided evidence of the discursive struggle that surrounds issue-oriented trials. At various times both the traditional and feminist understandings of rape have gained legitimacy or predominance. These two constructs have competed openly for attention in the public realm, each gaining coherent articulation in numerous ways and in a variety of texts. Seen in this light, there is cause for hope as well. Most significantly, as time has passed, mainstream news about rape trials has increasingly incorporated elements of the reformed understanding of rape. This trend should continue in future rape trial coverage. In two of the three cases examined, major elements of the reformed definition were incorporated into mainstream discourse and given widespread support. These adjustments must not be overlooked or discounted as insignificant. It is on this terrain that the concept of marital rape was granted widespread support, and it was on this terrain that victims were reframed as heroes for coming forward and testifying publicly at great personal cost.

Depictions in mass-mediated popular fiction provide more cause for optimism even as they perpetuate some of the same limiting biases as mainstream news. Popular fiction, in contrast to the news media, is able to portray a wide range of characters since it is not required to include only the certified opinions of official experts. Popular narratives further emphasize interpersonal drama to the extent that social ills become personal problems that are traceable to individual personalities and relationships. Neither mainstream news nor popular fiction offers a clear articulation of opposing systems of logic, but fiction does do a better job of rendering oppositional ideas in a coherent way, either by assigning them to particular characters or by including them in the personalities and motivations of the protagonist(s). Fiction also escapes the constraints of news with regard to narrative time; in fiction, the story can begin well before the beginning of the real news event and can extend beyond the point where the coverage ends.

The issue of rape is receiving unprecedented attention through the coverage of trials, and victims' experiences are gradually making their way into these mainstream discussions. The national discourse about rape trials is changing, and it increasingly includes expressions of support for ideas that just thirty years ago were not heard in public forums. Only by an outmoded and unrealistic standard could the effort of the rape law reform movement be considered a failure. In short, there is evidence that public opinion on the subject of rape is changing and that victims' voices have been heard. In the Rideout case, mainstream news incorporated nearly unanimous support for the idea that wives deserve protection from violent husbands, even though there was a decided lack of consensus on the question of how law could serve this practical purpose. In the Big Dan's case, mainstream news coverage frequently included expressions of support for the victim, and for the reform idea that personal characteristics such as welfare dependence and marital status are not relevant to consent and that women do not deserve or "ask for" brutal rape. Although the Dotson case was primarily one that defined ideological limits that reinforced traditional male fears about false imprisonment and the special nature of rape, it also included some explanation of feminist ideas in response to questions about victim veracity and trial procedures. In news coverage of all three cases, feminist experts were given an opportunity to comment, and such opportunities have expanded greatly between 1978 and 1985.

There is further cause for optimism when one looks at the responsiveness of mainstream discourse to the oppositional ideas of rape law reform. The very structures and values of news that are currently preventing rapid change may some day serve to accelerate it. The requirement of expert sources in particular offers a possibility for much more rapid change in the future, although it can be seen as a sort of check on the initial pace of such change: The emphasis on expert sources means that new ideas will be largely excluded from mainstream news until those ideas are accepted and articulated by the expert sources themselves. As more law students, professors, and district attorneys begin to understand and believe the rape reform view, these ideas will be articulated more frequently and coherently in mainstream news coverage that calls upon "expert" commentaries on specific cases.

In addition, as authors such as Helen Benedict continue to point out possibilities for improvement on the part of journalists covering such cases, conscientious reporters will effect change in their own work. Already the definition of "expert source" in the area of rape has expanded to include crisis counselors, rape survivors, and others beyond the principle attorneys in a particular case. Finally, as journalists become familiar with the ideas of rape law reform, these ideas will begin to receive a fair hearing in the news. Social change occurs through all of these processes, on the levels of individual identity and experience, and in the realms of subjectivity and discourse.

Public Trials in the Context of Social Change

Public trials are about power. They serve as the terrain on which, as Robert Hariman argues, opposing discourses do battle, and as such they are about the effort to determine definitions and truths central to our understanding of ourselves and our culture. Public trials are also about power in that their very existence is the result of conflict. In issue-oriented trials, social movements have won a place on the national agenda for their issues and concerns, and specific cases are taken up in the context of their struggle and arguments against mainstream ideas. Although it is not surprising that these crucial trials are not legally significant, or that they are not well suited to proving the validity of feminist views on rape, the importance of the prominence of these trials should not be underestimated. The existence of issue-oriented trials is itself an indicator of success: They reveal areas of discomfort and eventual change for dominant ideology. Issue-oriented trials treat subjects that disempowered groups wish to discuss. They serve as important sites of ideological accommodation because the terms in which they are discussed in the media are highly formalized and restricted and allow dominant ideology to adjust only at a measured pace.

Scholars of popular trials have noted that the rules of news writing converge in such a way that specific trials make good news because they offer an opportunity for "comparing and evaluating discourses before an audience of ordinary citizens" (Hariman 1990, 23). News coverage of these trials offers a chance for the dominant ideology to name the elements of the oppositional discourse that may be accepted as part of itself, while rendering mute or incoherent the rest of the opposing framework. As a result, in each of these three cases we did *not* see the clear articulation of the entire interrelated set of traditional ideas about rape or the whole set of reform views. Rather, we saw the acceptance of limited parts of rape reform discourse separated from the framework of meaning in which they were originally formulated.

Although this gives the illusion that such fragments of meaning can stand apart from the overall framework they represent, such fragmentation will continue to be problematic for public representations of rape. We cannot continue to believe both that rape is a "special crime" and that it is not, nor can we continue to believe both that women lie about rape and that they do not. Such contradictions have not been resolved, as discussions of rape trials have at times favored the idea that rape cases can be handled effectively by the jury system and at other times favored the notion that issues involving sex and emotion require special consideration.

All this should not be cause for undue dismay, for now that the issue of rape is on the national agenda and the struggle for meanings is well underway, the near future will bring more serious focus on rape-related trials. In news coverage of these subsequent trials we will witness the inclusion of increasing numbers of rape reform voices, as those voices become more mainstream. The three cases examined here spanned almost ten years and were the *first* highly publicized rape-oriented trials. It is not surprising that early trials on an issue would present incoherent, fragmented, and largely unsympathetic portrayals of the oppositional voice, but the existence of these trials is both a sign of change and an important opportunity for the articulation of that change. The official truth that emerges in the form of the trial verdict is not the end of the story. Social movements identify real inequities, and over time their reality is acknowledged. Significant social change is always slow, but highly publicized trials are a sign that some significant change is already underway.

The Gendered Nature of Public Discourses

Change happens faster in some areas than in others: The stories of these cases continued after the verdict and were rewritten in other forms, the most widely distributed of which have been the mass-mediated, constructed narratives examined in Chapter 5. If news portrayals are only tentative in their discussions of coherent oppositional viewpoints, fictional narratives are much more bold. While mainstream news selects particular "news worthy" elements for incorporation and virtually ignores the rest, fictionalized texts are more able to incorporate the entire position of rape law reform and to directly juxtapose it with the traditional view. Fictionalized narratives can pull the discussion in another direction, in favor of the female voice (though stopping short of suggesting a restructuring of society or power). Even though the fictionalized versions examined here also emerge within a patriarchal hegemony, and even though they do not suggest radical departures from business-as-usual, they nonetheless have in each case recuperated a female voice to a significant degree. While the role of mainstream news in issue-oriented trials is to provide a ground for the accommodation of dominant ideology to the challenges of oppositional discourse, the role of fiction is best seen as one of recuperation. Fiction exists as a second phase in the lengthy process of adjustment, one that takes up and extends salient issues from news coverage but adds new dimensions and interpretations. Perhaps it is not surprising that this recuperation takes place in a form considered "feminine": It is worth considering the implications of the gendered nature of the forms of news and popular fiction in this complicated process of social change.

As Rapping (1992), Radway (1984), and others have observed, certain popular forms, such as the romance and the television movie-of-the-week, can be considered feminine. They have primarily female audiences, are expressed in interpersonal terms and spaces, and depict the world from a largely female perspective that often includes overt criticism of patriarchal culture and its effects on women. In important ways, all of the fictionalized works examined here existed in feminine forms: The female-centered stories were all clearly addressed primarily to female audiences. It does not seem overly speculative to suppose that the (necessarily incomplete) sequestering of discourse types by gender is another means by which meanings and oppositional truths are contained and resisted. In other words, the truth of victims' experiences of rape are available more in fiction that addresses itself primarily to women than in news, which is a more masculine or at best ungendered form. Oppositional truths are again marginalized by the forum in which they find expression. This observation is not a new revelation, nor is it cause for despair. Rather, we are just beginning to understand the complexities entailed in the processes through which ideas of social change become widely accepted notions and truths.

Seen from one perspective, this marginalization of feminine[1] truth in the realms of fictional forms could be demoralizing, in that it might require both an unacceptable length of time for working feminist ideals into other forms and the possibility that two separate truths can coexist in "separate but equal" realms. The realities of form and content at present mean that fiction is better suited to the expression of female voices: It more easily enters and displays the private spaces traditionally inhabited by women. To the extent that this separation and coexistence of truths seems long-lived, it must also be seen as dangerous—an effective strategy for diffusion through marginalization or fragmentation. It cannot be denied that news exists as a more authoritative and legitimate source of knowledge than fiction.

However, seen from another perspective, the coexistence of two forms that express two versions of reality can be seen as a sign of both achievement and potential in the direction of social change. The existence of feminine forms in mass-mediated culture is evidence of the power of female audiences and, as we have seen, it allows for the coherent expression and legitimation of the female voice.

The dialectical nature of public discourse provides another reason for optimism. Fictional texts do not circulate in a vacuum, and they by no means reach only female audiences. Eventually, the truths expressed in fiction will find their way into news coverage of future trials. For now, it is primarily in fictionalized texts that victims' perspectives on rape are gaining national-level articulation. If our struggle is to gain voice by making the personalized political, it will continue to be necessary to bring the private into public discourse. However, fiction does not have the same authority as news to be the arbiter of mainstream ideology: Feminine forms such as romance novels and soap operas continue to be culturally devalued and even ridiculed as peripheral, unrealistic, or silly.

Chapter 3 states that the issue-oriented trial exists in special relation to the tension between powerful and disempowered groups, arguing that each genre of public trial has a unique role in relation to the exercise of power. One type represents the strategy of the disempowered or marginalized to make a point or gain public voice. Another represents the overt efforts of the existing power structure to purge itself of unruly or dangerous elements while reinforcing the legitimacy of its own power. A third serves primarily as entertainment and perhaps as a foil for the others: Celebrity cases may give the impression that important issues or struggles are being played out, while in fact most of the discussion revolves around the personality and history of the celebrity. Finally, the issue-oriented trial becomes highly publicized because previous efforts at change have placed an issue on the national agenda, indicating that oppositional groups and their ideas have gained some power. The oversights and overgeneralizations of this typology will be pointed out through further reflection and scholarship on these important trials.

The role of all public trials is centrally related to power and to the legitimation of those who hold it. Public discussion of these trials is about the power to define, to articulate, to speak and to be heard. Future scholarship on highly publicized trials should focus on their functioning as the attempts of various factions to exercise, maintain, or gain power. Issue-oriented trials should be studied in relation to movements for social change. They represent a later phase in the development of a social movement and are an indication of success at the deepest level of discourse and knowledge.

Future Directions

Future work on issue-oriented trials should continue to examine the process of presentation (news coverage) and re-presentation (post-trial fictionalization). In cases involving social change issues, it may actually be the fictionalized re-presentation (occurring after intense news coverage) that offers a forum for judging among discourses on a particular issue or set of issues by clearly articulating both sides. From the perspective of the agents of social change, then, the function of news may be to nominate and publicize particular cases that will later serve as the subject matter taken up and elaborated upon in other forms and forums.

There is also a trial-to-trial relationship that should be further investigated. Certain important contemporary issues, such as inner-city tensions and race relations, police brutality, the inclusion of gays in the military, and rape have been the subject of numerous trials. The discussions of trials that began to focus public attention on the issue in question must differ significantly from discussions of those that follow. Questions about when and why topics become the subjects of issue-oriented trials (and when and how they cease to warrant this type of national attention), the number and type of trials that ensue, and the general process of movement from initial to subsequent trials should be investigated in future research. Perhaps, by examining trials on issues that are no longer in the public eye, we can learn what sorts of resolutions or changes can be expected from our present struggles over meaning. We should also ask what factors influence the selection of certain cases for fictional treatment and whether the positions expressed in fiction find their way back into the news in subsequent cases.

This book has raised questions about how various discourses compare in their treatment of the same event or issue, but the delineations made between discourses here are arguably too broad: Further work of this type will undoubtedly draw distinctions between, for example, the various subtypes of news discourse as they operate on specific subject matter. Although much current scholarship focuses on mainstream news reporting, fewer insights are available on the different rhetorical mechanisms and ideological functions embedded within the forms of (for example) editorial, feature story, and syndicated columnist commentary. Each of these constitutes a distinct sub-genre of news discourse and is worthy of study. Also, points of comparison between Benedict's work and this study suggest that there may be significant differences between the content and role of local news and that of national news in processes of social change. Although the two in many ways cover the same themes within the same frameworks, their differences should be more thoroughly investigated.

This book is in part a record of the successes of rape law reformers in achieving a public voice for themselves and for the victims of rape. In many ways and in both forms of public discourse examined here, voices that articulate some part of the victim's experience of rape and traditional rape trials have been realized. There are many reasons for hope in looking toward the future of public discourses surrounding rape trials in the United States. The proliferation of cases that do not implicitly reinforce racist ideology (such as a trial involving a white rapist and black victim) and other traditional myths about rape will help in subtle ways to dispel the traditional myths and enable understanding of the reform construction. In addition, the movement of rape survivors and their supporters into positions from which their voices can be heard (as in journalism and law) will accelerate the movement of dominant ideology in the direction of the rape reform understanding.

Finally, although it may be a mistake to place much emphasis on the role of the voice of the individual survivor (if she speaks out only to be threatened and hounded out of town like the victim in the Big Dan's case), it is significant that victim voices are being heard and that victims are being encouraged to speak about their experiences in an overtly supportive environment. We must continue the fight to revalue all that is associated with the feminine, including feminine discourses (such as the popular fiction examined here), feminine themes (such as issues of power in interpersonal relationships), and the individual female voices of the survivors of dehumanizing experiences. As survivors and others speak out in ever greater numbers and denounce the traditional trial process as well as the culture that produces rape and rapists, a victim's perspective on rape will continue to gain credibility. Public trials provide one important platform from which this perspective can be expressed.

Note

1. Without intending to essentialize "feminine" and "masculine" as unified understandings, perspectives, or sets of experiences, I choose this language in order to call attention to the fact that certain truths are continually and systematically marginalized because of their critical content and their relation to the experiences of many women. The rape reform construction of rape has been such a perspective. There are important and widely shared elements of female experience that are marginalized or resisted, and these can accurately be labeled "feminine."

References

"Accused, The." 1988. Review of *The Accused*, screenplay by Tom Topor. *Variety*, 19 October, p. 14.

"Against a Wife's Will?" 1979. *Time* 1 January, p. 86.

Altschull, J. Herbert. 1984. *Agents of Power: The Role of the News Media in Human Affairs*. New York: Longman.

"Amid Outcry and Debate Over Judge's Decision, Man Resumes His Term for Rape." 1985. *New York Times*, 13 April, p. 1.

Amir, Menachem. 1967a. "Forcible Rape." *Federal Probation* 31: 51–58.

———. 1967b. "Victim Precipitated Forcible Rape." *Journal of Criminal Law, Criminology and Police Science* 58: 493–502.

———. 1971. *Patterns in Forcible Rape*. Chicago: University of Chicago Press.

Anderson, Hesper, Blue Andre, and Vanessa Greene. 1980. *Rape and Marriage: The Rideout Case* (screenplay). Lorimar Productions.

Barber, Susanna. 1985. "Big Dan's Rape Trial: An Embarrassment for First Amendment Advocates and the Courts." *Communications and the Law* (April): 3–21.

Baron, Larry, and Murray Strauss. 1989. *Four Theories of Rape in American Society: A State Level Analysis*. New Haven, CT: Yale University Press.

Beck, Melinda, and Marsha Zabarsky. 1984. "Rape Trial: Justice Crucified?" *Newsweek*, 2 April, p. 39.

Belknap, Michael R. 1981. *American Political Trials*. Westport, CT: Greenwood Press.

Benedict, Helen. 1992. *Virgin or Vamp: How the Press Covers Sex Crimes*. New York: Oxford University Press, 1992.

Beneke, Timothy. 1982. *Men on Rape*. New York: St. Martin's Press.

Bennett, W. Lance. 1988. *News: The Politics of Illusion*. New York: Longman.

"Big Dan's Tavern." 1984. *National Review*, 20 April, p. 20.

Black, Edwin. 1985. "Why Judge Samuels Sent Gary Dotson Back to Prison." *American Bar Association Journal* 71 (September): 56–59.

Black, Edwin, and Elizabeth Black. 1985. "The Unbelievable Case of Cathleen Webb." *Redbook* (October): 150–152.

Bonventre, Peter. 1979. "Was It Rape?" *Newsweek*, 1 January, p. 55.

Bourque, Linda Brookover. 1989. *Defining Rape*. Durham, NC: Duke University Press.

Bowers, John, and Donovan Ochs. 1971. *The Rhetoric of Agitation and Control.* London: Addison-Wesley.

Boyce, Bill. 1985. "Petition Drive Grows for Dotson." *Chicago Tribune*, 15 April, p. 2.1.

Brokaw, Tom. 6 February 1984. "NBC Nightly News."

———. 12 April 1985. "NBC Nightly News."

———. 17 May 1985. "NBC Nightly News."

Brownmiller, Susan. 1975. *Against Our Will: Men, Women and, Rape.* New York: Simon and Schuster.

Bumiller, Kristin. 1991. "Fallen Angels: The Representation of Violence Against Women in Legal Culture." In *At the Boundaries of Law*, edited by Martha Albertson Fineman and Nancy Sweet Thomadsen. New York: Routledge, 95–111.

Butterfield, Fox. 1991. "Charles Stuart's Brother Indicted in Murder Case." *New York Times*, 27 September 1991, A12.

———. "Trial of Six Starts Today in Pool Table Rape in Massachusetts." *New York Times*, 6 February, p. A6.

Byars, Jackie. 1991. *All that Hollywood Allows: Re-Reading Gender in 1950's Melodrama.* Chapel Hill: University of North Carolina Press.

Carter, Dan T. 1969. *Scottsboro: A Tragedy of the American South.* Baton Rouge: Louisiana State University Press.

"Case for a Spousal Rape Law, The." 1979. *Los Angeles Times*, 16 July.

"Child Abuse, Child Witnesses." 1990. *New York Times*, November 14, 16C.

Christenson, Ron. 1986. *Political Trials: Gordian Knots in the Law.* New Brunswick, NJ: Transaction Books.

"Commonwealth vs. John Cordeiro, Victor Raposo, Jose Madeiros, and Virgilio Madeiros. Continued Cross Examination of Cheryl A. Araujo by Attorney Judith L. Lindahl." *Bristol County Superior Court, Massachusetts* (Nos. 12267–68 and 13795–96).

"Commonwealth vs. Joseph Vieira and Commonwealth vs. Daniel C. Silva. Excerpt: Closing Arguments of Counsel." *Bristol County Superior Court, Massachusetts* (Nos. 12265–12266).

Condit, Celeste Michelle. 1990. *Decoding Abortion Rhetoric: Communicating Social Change.* Chicago: University of Illinois Press.

Connell, Noreen, and Cassandra Wilson, eds. 1974. *Rape: The First Sourcebook for Women.* New York: New American Library.

"Corroborating Charges of Rape." 1967. *Columbia Law Review* 67: 1137–1148.

"Court in New Bedford Hears Woman's Testimony." 1984. *New York Times*, 25 February, p. 12A.

Craik, Elizabeth. 1984. *Marriage and Property.* London: Aberdeen Press.

"Crimes and Crime Rates by Type." 1992. In *U.S. Statistical Abstracts*, Washington, DC: U.S. Department of Commerce, p. 180.

Currier, Frank. "CBS Evening News," 15 May 1983.

———. 2 March 1984. "CBS Evening News." (Transcript)

———. 11 April 1985. "CBS Evening News." (Transcript)

———. 27 March 1985. "CBS Evening News." (Transcript)

———. 16 May 1985. "CBS Morning News." (Transcript)

Daley, Steve. 1985. "Who's Using Whom in Dotson TV Flap?" *Chicago Tribune*, 19 May, p. 2.1.

"Defendant's Requested Jury Instructions." 1978. *Marion County Circuit Court* (No. 108,866).

"Defense Ends for One of Six in Rape Case." 1984. *New York Times*, 16 March, A11.

D'Emilio, John, and Estelle B. Freedman. 1988. *Intimate Matters: A History of Sexuality in America.* New York: Harper and Row.

"Different Focus." 1978. *San Francisco Journal,* 18 December, p. 7A.

Doody, Terrence. 1980. *Confession and Community in the Novel.* Baton Rouge: Louisiana State University Press.

Estrich, Susan. *Real Rape.* 1987. Cambridge, MA: Harvard University Press.

Evenson, Janet. 1978a. "Defense Argues that Mrs. Rideout Seeking 'Fame, Fortune' From Case." *Oregon Statesman Journal,* 21 December, p. 6C.

———. 1978b. "Defense Attorney's Questioning Challenges Mrs. Rideout's Honesty." *Oregon Statesman Journal,* December 23, p. 8A.

———. 1978c. "Jury Hears Views on Married Life of the Rideouts." *Oregon Statesman Journal,* 21 December, p. 1A.

———. 1978d. "Neighbor Tells of Screams at Rideout Residence." *Oregon Statesman Journal,* 23 December, p. 1A.

———. 1978e. "Rideout Neighbors Give Testimony." *Capital Journal,* 22 December, p. 8A.

———. 1978f. "Rideout Still Uncertain of Wife's Relationships." *Oregon Statesman Journal,* 27 December, p. 2A.

———. 1978g. "Rideout's Testimony: Wife's Description of Events, Husband's Description of Events." *Oregon Statesman,* 27 December, p. 6C.

———. 1978h. "Wife-Rape Trial: Threat to Husband Reported." *Oregon Statesman Journal,* 22 December, p. 1A.

Eyman, Joy Satterwhite. 1980. *How to Convict a Rapist.* New York: Stein and Day.

Faludi, Susan. 1991. *Backlash: The Undeclared War Against American Women.* New York: Crown.

Fawal, Joseph A. 1976. "Questioning the Marital Privilege: A Medieval Philosophy in a Modern World." *Cumberland Law Review* 7 (Fall): 307–322.

Fiske, John. 1989. *Reading the Popular.* Boston: Unwin Hyman.

Footlick, Jerrold. 1979. "Beating the Rape Rap." *Newsweek,* 8 January, p. 41.

"Forcible and Statutory Rape: An Exploration of the Operation and Objectives of the Consent Standard." 1952. *Yale Law Journal* 62: 55–83.

Frossard, Margaret. 1988. "When the Accuser Recants: People v. Dotson. *Litigation* 14.4 (Summer): 11–17.

Furey, John. 1978a. "Jurors Visit Rideout Apartment." *Capital Journal,* 20 December, p. 1A.

———. 1978b. "Mrs. Rideout Lied to Her Husband, 2 Witnesses Say." *Capital Journal,* 22 December, p. 1A.

———. 1978c. "Rideouts 'Have Both Suffered.'" *Capital Journal,* 28 December, p. 4A.

———. 1978d. "Witnesses Say Greta Expected Riches and Fame." *Capital Journal,* 21 December, p. 1A.

Gager, Nancy, and Cathleen Schurr. 1976. *Sexual Assault: Confronting Rape in America.* New York: Grossett and Dunlap.

Goldman, Peter, Tony Fuller, and Barbara Burgower. 1984. "New Bedford Rape: Rejecting the Myth." *Newsweek,* 26 March, p. 39.

Goodwin, Andrew, and Garry Whannel, eds. 1990. *Understanding Television.* New York: Routledge.

Gorney, Cynthia. 1979. "Behind Verdict in Rape Case." *Washington Post,* 1 January, p. 2.

Granger, Bill. "Lots to Admire in Dotson Case." 1985. *Chicago Tribune* 17 April, p. 2.1.

"Greta Rideout's Police Call Brought to Jury's Attention." 1978. *Capital Journal,* 21 December, 1B.

Griffin, Susan. 1979. *Rape: The Politics of Consciousness.* San Francisco: Harper and Row.

Groth, A. Nicholas. 1979. *Men Who Rape: The Psychology of the Offender.* New York: Plenum Press.

Hale, Sir Matthew. 1847. [1650]. *History of Pleas to the Crown, The.* Philadelphia: Robert H. Small.

Hariman, Robert, ed. 1990. *Popular Trials: Rhetoric, Mass Media, and the Law.* Tuscaloosa: University of Alabama Press.

Herman, Lawrence. 1977–78. "What's Wrong with the Rape Reform Laws?" *The Civil Liberties Review* (December/January): 60–74.

Hilberman, Elaine. 1976. *Rape Victim, The.* New York: Basic Books.

Holmstrom, Lynda L., and Ann Wolbert Burgess. 1978. *The Victim of Rape: Institutional Reactions.* New York: John Wiley and Sons.

Horos, Carol V. 1974. *Rape.* New Canaan, CT: Tobey Publishing.

Hursch, Carolyn J. 1977. *The Trouble with Rape.* Chicago: Nelson-Hall.

Jennings, Peter. 15 March 1984. "ABC World News Tonight."

————. 12 April 1985. "ABC World News Tonight."

Johnson, Brian D. 1988. "The Reality of Rape." Review of *The Accused,* screenplay by Tom Topor. *Macleans',* 24 October 1988, 60–62.

Juviler, Michael. 1960 "Psychiatric Opinions as to Credibility of Witnesses: A Suggested Approach." *California Law Review* 48: 648–683.

Kass, John, and Ann Marie Lipinski. 1985. "'Wronged Man' Gets Court Date." *Chicago Tribune,* 28 March, p. 1.1.

Kennedy, Royal. 1978. "ABC World News Tonight." 19 December.

————. 28 December 1978. "ABC World News Tonight."

Kivett, Lisa. 1986. "Sexual Assault: The Case for Removing the Spousal Exemption from Texas Law." *Baylor Law Review* 38: 1041–1062.

Kuralt, Charles. 1 April 1984. "CBS Morning News." (Transcript)

————. 19 May 1985. "CBS Sunday Morning." (Transcript)

Kurtis, Bill. 23 March 1984. "CBS Morning News." (Transcript)

————. 5 April 1985. "CBS Morning News." (Transcript)

————. 12 April 1985. "CBS Morning News." (Transcript)

————. 15 April 1985. "CBS Morning News." (Transcript)

————. 27 March 1985. "CBS Morning News." (Transcript)

Ledbetter, Les. 1978a. "Oregon Man Found Not Guilty of 1st-Degree Rape of His Wife." *New York Times,* 28 December, p. A1.

————. 1978b "Oregon Wife Testifies Husband Beat Her Before Rape." *New York Times,* 27 December, p. A14.

Lewin, Tamar. 1992. "Woman at Center of Debate: Model of an Ardent Feminist." *New York Times,* 1 July, p. A18.

Liddick, Betty. 1978. "Wife vs. Husband." *San Francisco Chronicle,* 11 December, p. 22.

Lipinski, Ann Marie. 1985. "She Looked So Good on TV: But on Witness Stand, Webb Lost Her Credibility." *Chicago Tribune,* 14 April, p. 2.1.

MacKellar, Jean. 1975. *Rape: The Bait and Trap.* New York: Crown.

Madigan, Lee, and Nancy Gamble. 1989. *The Second Rape: Society's Continued Betrayal of the Victim.* New York: Lexington Books.

"Marriage, Rape, and the Law." 1978. *New York Times,* 29 December, p. 22.1.

Marsh, Jeanne C., Alison Geist, and Nathan Caplan. 1982. *Rape and the Limits of Law Reform.* Boston: Auburn House.

Martin, Del. 1976. *Battered Wives.* San Francisco: Glide Press.

McGillis, Kelly. 1988. "Memoir of a Brief Time in Hell." *PeopleWeekly*, 14 November, pp. 154–160.

Medea, Andra, and Kathleen Thompson. 1974. *Against Rape.* New York: Farrar, Straus and Giroux.

"Memorandum of Law—Demurrer." 1978. *Marion County District Court* (No. 108,866).

"Memorandum in Support." 1984. *Bristol County Superior Court* (No. 12265).

Mitchell, Jan. 1978. "'Ordinary Couple' Split by Marital Rape Trial in Oregon." *San Francisco Chronicle*, 24 December, p. A8.

Mitra, Charlotte L. 1979. "For She Has No Right or Power to Refuse Her Consent." *Criminal Law Review* (September): 558–565.

Mydans, Seth. 1992. "Los Angeles Votes on Lenient Verdict." *New York Times*, 31 May, p. A13.

Myrdal, Gunnar. 1944. *An American Dilemma: The Negro Problem in Modern Democracy.* New York: Harper and Row.

"Oregon Rape Trial Puts Domestic Protection Law in the Dock." 1978. *Washington Post*, 18 December, p. A3.

Pauley, Jane. 15 May 1985. "The Today Show." *NBC.* (Transcript)

"People of the State of Illinois vs. Gary E. Dotson." *Circuit Court of Cook County, Illinois* (No. 77 I6 5200).

Petersen, Barry. 21 December 1978. "CBS Morning News." (Transcript)

———. 22 December 1978. "CBS Morning News." (Transcript)

Porter, Roy. 1986. "Rape: Does It Have a Historical Meaning?" In *Rape*, edited by Sylvana Tomaselli and Roy Porter, London: Basil Blackwell, 216–236.

Press, Aric et al. 1985. "Rape and the Law." *Newsweek*, 20 May, pp. 60–64.

Rangel, Jesus. 1984. "Portuguese Immigrants Fear Rape Case May Set Back Gains." *New York Times*, 17 March, p. 1.6.

———. 1984. "Rape Trial Is Monitored By a Women's Coalition." *New York Times*, 9 March, p. A10.

———. 1984. "Rape Trial Keeps Massachusetts Area on an Emotional Edge." *New York Times*, 4 March, p. 22.

"'Rape Law' Changed by Oregon Solons." 1978. *Oregon Journal*, 25 December, p. A2.

"Rape in Marriage." 1979. *San Francisco Chronicle* 14 January, p. 1.

"Rape: New Controversy on Old Issue." 1985. *U.S. News and World Report*, 27 May, p. 52.

"Rape? No: Wife Loses." 1979. *Time*, 8 January, p. 61.

"Rape—Or a Marital Tiff?." 1978. *Oakland Tribune*, 27 December, p. D2.

Rapping, Elayne. 1992. *The Movie of the Week: Private Stories, Public Events.* American Culture, vol. 6. Minneapolis, MN: University of Minnesota Press.

Raspberry, William. 1979. "Reconciliation and the Rideouts." *Oakland Tribune*, 17 January, p. 32.

Rather, Dan. 24 February 1984. "CBS Evening News." (Transcript)

———. 12 April 1985. "CBS Evening News." (Transcript)

———. 11 May 1985. "CBS Evening News." (Transcript)

"Readers Favor a Rape Law." 1979. *San Francisco Chronicle*, 11 January, p. 1.

Rede, George. 1978a. "The Background." *Capital Journal*, 22 December, p. 1C.

———. 1978b. "Both Sides Praise Judge's Decision." *Capital Journal*, 28 December, p. 1C.

Reiner, Cynthia. 1978. "Rideout Acquittal Saddens Feminists." *Capital Journal*, 28 December, p. 1C.

"Reply Memorandum of Joseph Vieira." 1984. *Bristol County Superior Court* (No. 12265).

"Reports to Police Questioned." 1984. *New York Times,* 22 March, p. A18.

"Revolution in Rape, A." 1979. *Time,* 2 April, p. 50.

"Rideout Case Shows Limitations of System." 1979. *Oregon Statesman Journal,* 29 December, p. 6D.

"Rideouts' Home Life Described." 1978. *Capital Journal,* 21 December, p. 1A.

Rosenberg, Martin. 1978. "John Rideout Is Relieved It's Over." *Capital Journal,* 18 December, p. 1A.

Russell, Diana E. H. 1975. *The Politics of Rape: The Victim's Perspective.* New York: Stein and Day.

————. *Rape in Marriage.* 1982. New York: MacMillan.

Sanders, William B. 1980. *Rape and Women's Identity.* Sage Library of Social Research, vol. 106. Beverly Hills: Sage.

Savage, Audrey. 1990. *Twice Raped.* Indianapolis, IN: Book Weaver Publishing.

Sawyer, Diane. 1984. "CBS Morning News." 19 March.

————. 22 March 1984. "CBS Morning News."

Schanberg, Sydney. 1984. "The Rape Trial." *New York Times* 27 March, p. A31.

Schiff, Arthur Frederick. 1979. "State of Oregon v. Rideout- Can Husband Rape Wife?" *Medical Trial Technique Quarterly* 26 (Summer): 49–56.

Schuetz, Janice, and Kathryn Holmes Snedaker. 1988. *Communication and Litigation: Case Studies of Famous Trials.* Carbondale: Southern Illinois University Press.

Serrill, Michael. 1985. "Cathy and Gary in Medialand." *Time,* 27 May, p. 66.

"Shame in New Bedford and Dallas." 1984. *New York Daily News,* 28 March, p. A26.

Shipp, E. R. 1985a. "Foster Parents Contradict Woman Who Says Rape Didn't Happen." *Chicago Tribune,* 11 May, p. 11.

————. 1985b. "Prosecutors in Disputed Rape Case See Trail of Contradictions." *New York Times,* 18 April, p. A14.

————. 1985c. "Testimony Challenges Woman Who Recanted in Rape Charge." *New York Times,* 12 May, p. 20.

Simpson, Antony E. 1986. "The 'Blackmail Myth' and the Prosecution of Rape and Its Attempt in 18th Century London: The Creation of a Legal Tradition." *Journal of Criminal Law and Criminology* 77 (Spring): 101–150.

Southern, David. 1987. *Gunnar Myrdal and Black-White Relations: The Use and Abuse of "An American Dilemma."* Baton Rouge: Louisiana State University Press.

Starr, Mark. 1984. "Gang Rape: The Legal Attack." *Newsweek,* 12 March, p. 38.

Starr, Mark, and Patricia King. 1985. "Who Is the Real Victim?" *Newsweek,* 20 May, pp. 69–73.

Starr, Mark, and Frank Maier. 1985. "More Than a Case of Rape." *Newsweek,* 22 April, p. 21.

Sternoff, Bill. 19 December 1978. "NBC Nightly News."

————. 22 December 1978. "NBC Nightly News."

————. 27 December 1978. "NBC Nightly News."

Sussman, Les, and Sally Bordwell. 1981. *The Rapist File.* New York: Chelsea House.

Swanson, Stevenson. 1985. "Redefining Society's Perceptions of Rape." *Chicago Tribune,* 2 June, p. 2.1.

Taylor, Julie. 1987. "Rape and Women's Credibility: Problems of Recantations and False Accusations Echoed in the Case of Cathleen Crowell Webb and Gary Dotson." *Harvard Women's Law Journal* 10 (Spring): 59–116.

Thompson, Mildred. 1990. *Ida B. Wells-Barnett: An Exploratory Study of an American Black Woman, 1893–1930.* Brooklyn, NY: Carlson Publishing Company.

Topor, Tom. *The Accused* (screenplay). Paramount Pictures, 1988.

Touraine, Alain. *Return of the Actor*. Minneapolis: University of Minneapolis Press, 1988.

"Trial Memorandum." 1978. *Marion County Circuit Court* (No. 108,866).

"Two Rape Trial Witnesses Declare Accuser Lied." 1978. *New York Times*, 23 December, p. 10.5.

van Dijk, Teun. 1988. *News as Discourse*. Hillsdale, NJ: Lawrence Erlbaum.

Vespa, Mary. 1984. "No Town Without Pity, A Divided New Bedford Seeks Justice in a Brutal Case of Gang Rape." *PeopleWeekly*, March, pp. 77–81.

Victimology. 1978. Special Issue. v. 2.3–2.4. Ed. Emelio Viano.

Walker, Marcia J., and Stanley L. Brodsky. 1976. *Sexual Assault*. Lexington, MA: D.C. Heath.

Warshaw, Robin. 1988. *I Never Called It Rape: The Ms. Report on Recognizing, Fighting and Surviving Date and Acquaintance Rape*. New York: Harper and Row.

Webb, Cathleen. 1985. "Trying to Make It Right." *PeopleWeekly*, 29 April, pp. 36–42.

Webb, Cathleen, and Marie Chapian. 1987. *Forgive Me*. Tappan, NJ: Revell.

"Wife Has No Regrets." 1978. *Capital Journal*, 30 December.

"Wife's Credibility at Issue in Rape." 1978. *San Francisco Chronicle*, 22 December, p. 22.

Wigmore, John Henry. 1942. *Evidence in Trials at Common Law*. 3d ed. Boston: Little, Brown.

Will, George. 1978. "Does Oregon's Rape Law Go Too Far?" *Capital Journal*, 29 December.

"Woman Recants Rape Charge Six Years Later." 1985. *New York Times*, 30 March, p. L6.

Wriggins, Jennifer. 1983. "Rape, Racism, and the Law." *Harvard Women's Law Journal* 6: 103–141.

Index

University of Pennsylvania Press
Feminist Cultural Studies, the Media, and Political Culture
Mary Ellen Brown and Andrea Press, Editors

Lisa M. Cuklanz. *Rape on Trial: How the Mass Media Construct Legal Reform and Social Change.* 1996

Margaret J. Heide. *Television Culture and Women's Lives:* thirtysomething *and the Contradictions of Gender.* 1995

Dana Heller. *Family Plots: The De-Oedipalization of Popular Culture.* 1995

Andrea Press. *Women Watching Television: Gender, Class, and Generation in the American Television Experience.* 1991

This book was set in Baskerville and Eras typefaces. Baskerville was designed by John Baskerville at his private press in Birmingham, England, in the eighteenth century. The first typeface to depart from oldstyle typeface design, Baskerville has more variation between thick and thin strokes. In an effort to insure that the thick and thin strokes of his typeface reproduced well on paper, John Baskerville developed the first wove paper, the surface of which was much smoother than the laid paper of the time. The development of wove paper was partly responsible for the introduction of typefaces classified as modern, which have even more contrast between thick and thin strokes.

Eras was designed in 1969 by Studio Hollenstein in Paris for the Wagner Typefoundry. A contemporary script-like version of a sans-serif typeface, the letters of Eras have a monotone stroke and are slightly inclined.

Printed on acid-free paper.